Federal, State, and Local
Government in Education

Federal, State, and Local Government in Education

42059

TRUMAN M. PIERCE

Dean, School of Education
Auburn University

The Center for Applied Research in Education, Inc.
New York

Second Printing... September, 1965

LIBRARY OF CONGRESS
CATALOG CARD NO.: 64-20121

PRINTED IN THE UNITED STATES OF AMERICA

Foreword

Federal, State, and Local Government in Education, by Dr. Truman M. Pierce, traces the expanding role of government at all levels in American education. The origin and development of various educational services by the different branches of government are reviewed. The viewpoint throughout the book is that education under the auspices of government has both reflected and strengthened the growth and implementation of basic concepts of individual freedom and opportunity which motivated early framers of our government.

The reader senses a lack of coordination among the three levels of government in the origin and growth of the American public school system. Extensive local freedom has been cherished which has brought rewards through stimulating initiative and self-confidence in individual communities, but in some instances it may have been wasteful of resources. Although there are fifty separate state school systems, much nationwide integration of education has taken place through teacher preparation, professional organizations and journals, accreditation, textbook publishers and state adoptions, and migration of teachers. Some of these developments are specifically provided for by government. Others are encouraged by freedom which individuals and groups are permitted to exercise. Such developments are paralleled in several aspects of our culture.

The reader senses, too, that with the great capacity of the country to produce material goods for the support of education or for other purposes, growing concern relates to developing more effectively staff and learner potential through closer cooperation among levels of government and agents concerned with education. Increasing interdependence in American education and culture emphasize the need for speeding up the reevaluation of the educational roles of government and of improved coordination among its branches. The scope and analytical approach of Dr. Pierce outlines the legal background for a possible speedup. Organization of the book makes it easy to follow the major thought.

Many school administrators, teachers, and laymen have meager understandings of present relationships between government and education in the United States, and of consequences which might accompany different avenues of further development. The book should be a timely asset to all such persons.

HAROLD H. PUNKE
Professor of Education
Auburn University

Contents

CHAPTER I

Introduction

The relationships of government to education in the United States stem from no conceptual design. Their origins lie in the use of government by the people as an instrument for achieving goals sought through education. These goals are deeply rooted in the American ideals of concern for the welfare of all people, and the belief that the government exists to serve the best interests of all of them.

The American public school system has been shaped by many influences. The impact of government has been and is increasingly the strongest force in its development. Indeed, the evolution of governmental relations to education is now at the stage where full responsibility for public education is placed with the government. A brief review of some of the reasons which led to the founding of this country will provide perspective essential to an understanding of the role of government in education.

A variety of conditions led to the colonization of America—one led to the search for freedom, and gave vitality to the development of the new world. This search was complex and its specifics included the desire (1) to worship according to the dictates of one's conscience, (2) to escape from oppression by government, (3) to escape from political persecution, and (4) to search for an unrestricted opportunity to make one's own way in life. This emphasis on individual freedom was a powerful force in the establishment of the United States of America and is paramount in our early political documents.

This concept of human worth was scarcely dignified by the structure and control of colonial governments. But the spirit of freedom was strong and by 1775 the thirteen colonies were determined to assume responsibility for their own destiny. Winning the War for Independence paved the way for a new experiment in government.

The social institutions that developed in the colonies reflected in many ways the ideals and aspirations held by the people, some of which were unique to the new world. Concern for the nature and

1

function of government and the relationships of government to the rights of the individual were evident in the colonies. Belief in education was strong and efforts were soon directed toward the provision of educational opportunities in the new land.

The colonists naturally brought with them views on education which prevailed in their native lands. Hence, there was wide acceptance of the view that providing and operating schools was a legitimate function of the church. Most of the early colleges and universities were established, supported, and largely controlled by the church as were some of the lower schools. The church furthered its own purposes and philosophy through the curricula of its schools.

Private schools were also established at this time, as were the academies. Their curricula were generally broader than those of the church schools and were oriented more toward the practical and functional—the utilitarian values of education. Other types of private schools grew, which served such purposes as their founders deemed important.

A third educational development in the colonies was the beginning of a public school system. Several colonies attempted to support schools financially through local taxes and state funds. As early as 1642 Massachusetts passed an educational act similar in some respects to the old English Apprenticeship Law which provided for industrial education: but this act also recognized other purposes of education. A law was passed by this colony in 1647 which required a town of fifty families to maintain an elementary school and each town of one hundred families to maintain, in addition, a grammar (secondary) school. A town tax rate was prescribed, but provision was also made for the support of these schools by tuition fees and grants. A number of other colonies took steps to encourage public schools.

There was also from the start of colonization a strong belief that education provided a way for the individual to improve his position in life. This belief has since become a part of our national philosophy. Much of the federal government's concern for education has been reflected in decisions designed to help provide the kinds of learning which make individuals more secure economically. The meaning of this concept has also passed through various stages of evolution.

Historically, Americans have always viewed education as an instrument for the common good as well as for individual enhancement. This concept is closely related to making democracy work and to creating for the individual the best opportunities for his advancement. This point of view has led to the use of government as a positive influence for social betterment, since individual and social enhancement go hand in hand.

The new government created after the Revolution was devised for the purpose of serving both individual welfare and the common welfare to the highest degree possible. The new government was both an expression of the ideals of a people and the creation of an instrument for achieving these ideals to a higher degree.

The Declaration of Independence defines regard for the individual and the role of government in the following words:

> We hold these truths to be self-evident, that all men are created equal, that they are endowed by their Creator with certain inalienable Rights, that among these are Life, Liberty, and the pursuit of Happiness.
>
> That, to secure these rights, Governments are instituted among Men, deriving their just powers from the consent of the governed, . . .

The philosophy of government implicit in this statement and the belief in education were powerful factors in the development of the United States.

Hence, by the time the colonies won their freedom and established the United States of America, the people had demonstrated their interest in and concern for education by the establishment of three distinctive types of schools. The church and private schools were not a responsibility of government. The third type, the public school, was the immediate concern of government and is the beginning of the modern public school system in this country. Dedication to education, belief in its power, and concepts of how it should be provided were extended into the new national government.

Herein originated a new concern for education expressed by Thomas Jefferson in his belief that people could not govern themselves successfully unless they were educated. Thus, Jefferson favored a strong public school system open to everyone. Use of education as a force to make democracy work is evident throughout our national history. This concept has gone through several stages of evolution—from Jefferson's idea that if the people were to vote intelligently they must be educated to recognition of education as a means of survival in a world of competing ideologies. This point of view, too, has been a powerful factor in helping to shape the role of government in education throughout our national history.

The government of a democracy is an active agent of change. It exists to serve the people and not to be served by the people. A democratic society is a changing society because it encourages individual initiative and creativity. As long as man uses his intelligence productively, a democratic culture will be in a state of change. It will move toward a more adequate realization of its aspirations. Hence, government in a democracy cannot be static. Its specific functions and immediate goals will change as the needs of the people it serves change.

The ideals and aspirations of a democracy not only give direction to its change but also provide for essential stability. While change is always in progress, it stems from the present and the past and thus is at a given moment a point on the continuum of a society in transition. Since education is a chief agent of change, it has been of continuous interest to our government at all levels.

Before specifically undertaking the task of analyzing the relationships of government to education, a review of the structure of the American government is essential. Considerations of the functions ascribed to government and the interrelationships within and among governments are also necessary.

The Constitution provides for three branches of government with each having distinct functions. The three branches provide a system of checks and balances designed to preserve the democratic form of government and to assure its proper use. The legislative branch has authority and responsibility for making laws, providing funds for government use, and approving appointments. The executive branch is charged with the administrative functions of government and with responsibilities for policy-making. The judicial branch is designed to see that the government functions as intended by the Constitution and to protect the rights of the people from usurpation by government or denial by others. Each branch of government has authority to play a role in education, but the roles are different and should be examined separately. These roles are in many respects supplementary to each other.

The pattern established by the federal government has been used as a model by state governments. Each state also has executive, legislative, and judicial branches. State constitutions outline in varying degrees the respective powers, responsibilities, and duties of these three branches of government but their interrelationships correspond roughly to those of the three branches of the federal government. Responsibilities to and concern for education vary among these three branches of government from state to state. It is necessary to study these responsibilities and relationships in order to understand the relationship of government to education.

To a lesser degree, the three-branch concept has also been developed in local government, particularly in cities. The mayor or city manager is the chief executive, the city council, or a similar body, has legislative functions, and the larger cities have judicial systems. County, town governments, and other local governments have imitated this pattern but less clearly and with more variations. The three branches of government on a local level may each influence education, but the pattern of influence is difficult to trace because of numerous local variations from state to state and within states.

The analysis of governmental relationships to education is, therefore, far from simple, since three levels of government and three branches at each level must be considered. There is also the further complex problem of tracing the interacting relationships of the three levels of government as they have affected education. The roles of the three levels of the federal government are easier to analyze because there are fifty state school systems, each with factors unique to its own system.

Summary

Historical perspective has been sketched as a basis for analysis of the relationships of government to education. The value context in which public education in America has developed largely accounts for these relationships. Public schools evolved slowly in this country.

The American government is unique in character and function and it has always been viewed as an instrument for the common good. A democracy tends to stimulate change because the needs of people it serves change. The values and aspirations basic to a democracy provide the dynamics of change. In this country, more than in any other country, until recent years, education has been used to bring about individual enhancement and social good.

The importance attached to education is reflected by the role of government in establishing and maintaining schools. Federal, state, and local government have their respective roles in educational affairs. Furthermore, the executive, legislative and judicial branches of each level of government each have their impact on education.

The next chapter describes and analyzes provisions of the federal and the state constitutions which have influenced education.

CHAPTER II

Constitutional Provisions for Education

The constitution of a nation or state is the basic law under which it functions. Constitutions may be written or unwritten. The written type sets forth the structure, powers, and duties of a government while the unwritten type consists of a collection of acts or documents of a governing body which become precedents. The former type of constitution can be modified or changed only by the processes set forth in the document itself while the latter can be changed by action of the governing body. The United States Constitution belongs to the former type. The constitution of Great Britain is of the latter type.

The written constitution is more stable than the unwritten type since procedures for its amendment are usually designed to prevent hasty or ill-advised change or change supported only by simple majority opinion. Important constitutional change can be brought about, in effect, by the judiciary which has the power to interpret the meanings of constitutional provisions. Interpretations vary according to the personnel of the judiciary and the prevailing social and economic context. Hence, even the written type of constitution may be amenable to the ever-changing cultural conditions, attitudes, and values.

There are three kinds of basic legal documents under which American people are governed. The first is the Federal Constitution which takes precedence over the other two and which demands that their provisions be consistent with its own. State constitutions are the second type of constitutional documents and the third type—under which Americans in municipalities are governed—is the charter granted by the state. These documents must have no provisions which run contrary to either the state or Federal Constitutions. People who do not live in a municipality live under local governments authorized by either the state constitution or the state legislature under general prescriptions.

7

Each type of constitutional document has some relationship to education. It will be necessary, therefore, to discuss all three types.

The Federal Constitution

The United States Constitution is a unique document. The system of checks and balances which it prescribes is one example of uniqueness, as is its extensive plan for government. Perhaps its greatest contribution lies in the basic philosophy which the document sets forth. This philosophy is eloquently stated in the preamble as follows:

> We, the people of the United States, in Order to form a more perfect Union, establish Justice, insure domestic Tranquillity, provide for the common defence, promote the general Welfare, and secure the Blessings of Liberty to ourselves and our Posterity, do ordain and establish this Constitution for the United States of America.

Here, purposes to be served by the new government are stated in unmistakable language. These purposes are in effect a restatement of the philosophy of the Declaration of Independence. It is clear that the new government was to be the servant of the people.

There is no reference in the Constitution to education, nor do any of the several amendments concern themselves with education. However, the lack of mention is not to be construed as lack of interest on the part of convention delegates.

Winning the war for independence did not have any early effect on education. The three types of schools briefly described were accepted by the people as a part of the new national life. Apparently, adoption of the Constitution without mention of education merely indicates that the new nation felt no need to change the existing provisions for schools.

Between 1776 and 1800 only five of fourteen state constitutions made reference to education. By 1800 eight of the sixteen states in the Union had adopted constitutions which made no reference to education. Some of these states, however, were pioneers in the development of public schools, notably New York and Connecticut. Their constitutions, as revised later, did refer to education.

There was discussion of education in the constitutional convention but other matters for which there was less precedent demanded more of the time and energy of the delegates. There were individuals in the convention who did not believe in educating the masses. They were known as Federalists, and stood for a highly centralized government and a society in which education was reserved largely for the elite. On the other hand, some delegates favored education for the masses. There was also an element in the convention which took the position that the church and not the government should have responsibility for education.

It may be that under these conditions those in the convention who were strong advocates for public education decided it was better to settle for the document as finally adopted. The implied powers of the new government provided sufficient opportunity to safeguard the interests of those who believed in education for everyone.

In spite of the lack of reference to education in the Constitution, certain sections have had a profound impact on the public schools of this country. Among these sections are the following.

The General Welfare Clause. Article I, Section 8, of the Federal Constitution states that:

> The Congress shall have Power: To lay and collect Taxes, Duties, Imposts and Excises, to pay the Debts and provide for the common Defence and general welfare of the United States; but all Duties, Imposts and Excises shall be uniform throughout the United States; ...

As stated earlier, Americans have viewed education as being of paramount importance in providing for the welfare of the people. This part of our national philosophy has assumed increasing importance, and it seems safe to say that historically America has not felt that the welfare of her people could be adequately safeguarded and assured without a system of education. The clause, as it has been interpreted, authorizes the United States government to levy and collect revenues which can be used for the support of education. The extent of this support depends on the Congress.

Decisions under the general welfare clause affecting education most profoundly have been court decisions. Several such decisions have been made by the Supreme Court, some of which will be considered in a later chapter. (See Chapter V.)

The general welfare clause has also been interpreted by some to give the Congress of the United States the power to establish and support a federal system of education. The Supreme Court probably would have to determine the constitutionality of any such authorization.

Implied powers.   Article X of the Bill of Rights says that: "The powers not delegated to the United States by the Constitution, nor prohibited by it to the States, are reserved to the states respectively, or to the people."

This article has greatly influenced the pattern of American government, including government relations to education. Had a strict interpretation of the Constitution been substituted for this amendment, the federal government would have been empowered to do only that which was specifically authorized by the Constitution. The government's relationship to education would have been eliminated until such time as the Constitution might have been changed.

The Tenth Amendment made education a function of the states and subsequent federal support for education has acknowledged this principle in the main. It should be noted that nowhere were the states directed to accept responsibility for education. However, it is a matter of record that each state in the Union has accepted this responsibility and acted accordingly in the establishment and support of a state school system. The development of the public school system in America is the story of an increasing assumption of this responsibility by the states from generation to generation.

Due process of law.   The experiences of the colonists with the English government and with colonial governments made them very sensitive to the importance of constituting a government that could not infringe on rights of the citizens. This point is the central concern of the Bill of Rights, the first ten amendments to the Constitution.

The manner in which citizens are to be protected against government usurpation of their rights is set forth in Article V of the Bill of Rights. It reads:

> No person shall be held to answer for a capital, or otherwise infamous crime ... except in cases arising in the land or naval forces, or in the Militia, when in actual service in time of War or public danger; nor shall any person be subject for the same offence to be twice put in jeopardy of life or limb; nor shall be compelled in any criminal case to be a witness against himself, nor be deprived of life, liberty, or property, without due process of law; nor shall private property be taken for public use without just compensation.

Upon first examination, this amendment's relevance to education may not be clear. In one sense, the amendment obligates the federal government to protect the rights of its citizens. If the right to an education is included among these rights, then its significance for government relationships to education is clear. The amendment restrains the government from infringing upon those rights of citizens which are guaranteed by the Constitution. Protection of the citizen against his own government is a function of the courts. When certain court decisions are examined, the relationship will be more obvious. These decisions will be presented in a later chapter.

Restriction of states with respect to rights of individual citizens. As the United States developed, it became clear that although the federal government had adequately safeguarded the rights of citizens in its constitutional provisions, some state constitutions had not done so in all cases. At the conclusion of the Civil War, the Fourteenth Amendment to the Constitution was adopted to cover this point. The amendment reads as follows:

> All persons born or naturalized in the United States, and subject to the jurisdiction thereof, are citizens of the United States and of the State wherein they reside. No State shall make or enforce any law which shall abridge the privileges or immunities of citizens of the United States; nor shall any State deprive any person of life, liberty, or property, without due process of law; nor deny to any person within its jurisdiction the equal protection of the laws.

This amendment is of profound significance to schools and education as court cases falling under its provisions are decided by the Supreme Court. It is the legal basis under which the dual school system of the southern states was attacked. Under this amendment, the Supreme Court struck down the separate but equal doctrine which supported racial segregation in the public schools.

Separation of church and state. The concept of separation of church and state is an outstanding example of how the new government was designed to protect citizens against types of oppression and discrimination to which they had been subjected in the past. Since many colonists came to America in search of religious freedom, it is not surprising to see this doctrine stated in the basic law of the land. It reads:

> Congress shall make no law respecting an establishment of religion, or prohibiting the free exercise thereof; or abridging the free-

dom of speech, or of the press; or the right of the people peaceably to assemble, and to petition the Government for a redress of grievances.

The significance of this amendment as it applies to schools has never been fully determined. Generally speaking, the amendment has been interpreted to mean that the public schools must be non-sectarian. It has also been interpreted to mean that the federal government cannot support church schools and that public schools cannot foster a particular religion. There is at present a question concerning the right of the public school to deal with religion in any way.

State Constitutions

The various states have been free to develop their own systems of public education because the Constitution states that powers not specifically delegated to the federal government nor withheld from the states may be exercised by the states. Theoretically, it would seem a state might have chosen not to provide schools. However, this could be questioned under the general welfare clause. Historically, however, each state assumed the responsibility for establishing and maintaining a public school system.

Actually the states had no option in the matter, for belief in public education was too firmly established. Congress has, on more than one occasion, required a territory requesting admission to the Union to make provision in its constitution for the establishment and maintenance of public schools. The role of the federal government has been that of helping the states when it chose so to do. States have been free to exercise all leeway possible short of violating provisions of the Constitution.

Fifty state school systems. There is no American public school system as such; instead, there are fifty state public school systems. No federal system of education with its possible evils has been developed. The uniformity and central control of such a system would have done violence to the American concept of local initiative in education. It might also have done harm to the philosophy that schools should be sensitive to the educational needs unique to the communities they serve. Under decentralized control, school systems have been able to adapt to local and regional needs. Such variability is conducive to the healthy diversity which a democracy should encourage.

Each state constitution defines the authority and responsibility for the development and support of public schools within its borders, but provisions vary greatly from state to state. A study of state constitutional provisions is essential to an adequate understanding of our public schools. An attempt is made in the following pages to classify these provisions in a general way.

Defining educational purpose and state responsibility. The values ascribed to education commonly held by the American people and their leaders are generally reflected in constitutional stipulations. Article II, Section 12, of the Tennessee Constitution states that:

> Knowledge, learning and virtue, being essential to the preservation of republican institutions, and the diffusion of the opportunities and advantages of education throughout the different portions of the State being highly conducive to the promotion of this end, it shall be the duty of the General Assembly, in all future periods of this Government to cherish literature and science.

The Constitution of Delaware states in Article 10, Section 1, that: "The General Assembly shall provide for the establishment and maintenance of a general and efficient system of free public schools. . . ." Evidently, the function of the system of free public schools was assumed in this document.

Article 8, Section 1, of the Indiana Constitution states:

> Knowledge and learning, generally diffused throughout the community, being essential to the preservation of a free government, it shall be the duty of the General Assembly to encourage, by all suitable means, moral, intellectual, scientific, and agricultural improvement; and to provide, by law, for a general and uniform system of Common Schools, wherein tuition will be without charge, and equally open to all.

Considerable emphasis is placed in this statement on schools being open to all without charge to the pupil or his parents.

The Constitution of Texas states in Article 7, Section 1:

> A general diffusion of knowledge being essential to the preservation of the liberties and rights of the people, it shall be the duty of the legislature of the State to establish and make suitable pro-

vision for the support and maintenance of an efficient system of public free schools.

The Constitution of the State of New York in Article 11, Section 1, merely states that: "The legislature shall provide for the maintenance and support of a system of free common schools, wherein all the children of the State may be educated."

The Constitution of Montana states in Article 11, Section 1: "It shall be the duty of the legislative assembly of Montana to establish and maintain a general, uniform and thorough system of public, free, and common schools."

Evidently the value of an education was so generally accepted that no reference to the function of these schools was deemed essential in the constitutions of some states. It will be noted that the term "common schools" is frequently used. The phrase seems to mean schools available to everyone irrespective of his means or station in life.

This somewhat random sample of provisions in state constitutions for the establishment of public schools and the purposes to be served thereby are fairly typical of the fifty state constitutions. How purposes were to be achieved was in some cases left almost wholly to the state legislatures; in other cases, means and procedures were described in additional constitutional provisions.

Organization and administration of education at the state level. A structure for the public school system is set forth for each state either by constitutional provision or legislative enactment. This was essential if the legislature was to successfully execute the duties given by its state constitution. Some plan of organizing and administering the public schools from the state level was obviously needed. New agencies and new official positions in state governments were therefore created.

All states have provided for a head of their public school systems known generally as the state superintendent of schools. Other states designate this official as the Commissioner of Education. In West Virginia, he is the State Superintendent of Free Schools. More than half of the state constitutions have made this a constitutional office, while in the rest it is a legislative office.

A number of state constitutions mandate the creation of a state board of education. In some cases, the number of members of the board is specified in the constitution, with its functions defined in varying degrees. The state board of education in other states is created by the legislature.

Local organization and administration of schools. One of the unique contributions of the American system of education is the local school district, a plan of organization for providing education to local communities. No state has chosen to operate a completely centralized system of public education although the degree of decentralization varies considerably from state to state. Instead, the local school district has been invented. It is a creature of the state and is in essence an arm of the state reaching into the local community. One of the extraordinary aspects of this invention is that while the district is legally a creature of the state, operationally it functions in many respects as a creature of the local community.

Many constitutional provisions for local school districts are concerned with county school districts and the county superintendent of schools. A number of state constitutions set forth the manner of selection, qualifications, and term of office of this official. In other states, determining the local organization and administration of schools is left to the legislature.

Responsibility for financial support. One of the early acts of the federal government was the granting of public lands to the respective states for the purpose of supporting common schools.

Nearly half of the state constitutions prescribe the manner in which funds from the sale of school lands are to be invested and managed. More than half prescribe the manner in which these funds are to be apportioned, and an even larger number declare that public school funds, state or local, cannot be spent for sectarian purposes.

Many constitutions go further and make additional provisions for financing education. References are frequently made to gifts for educational purposes and to taxation for school support.

Alabama, for example, has a constitutional amendment providing that income tax be used for educational purposes. Or, specific taxes may be earmarked for education. The constitutions in about twenty states limit the tax rate on property for school purposes. The only way a school district can tax itself beyond such a limit is to secure approval of a constitutional amendment raising or removing the tax ceiling. The West Virginia Constitution classifies property for school tax purposes and specifies a ceiling on the tax rate for each classification.

Some state constitutions place a limit on the bonding power of a school district. The limitation is usually expressed in the form of a percentage of the assessed property valuation of the school district.

Delegation of authority to state legislatures. Constitutions generally empower state legislatures to maintain and support schools. This authorization implements the doctrine of education as a function of the state. It permits legislatures to exercise their own initiative and judgment without the possibility of unhealthy strictures caused by specific constitutional provisions. Great leeway is available to state legislatures and, as a consequence, many variations in practice occur. These variations are subject only to constitutional limits, state and federal, as interpreted by the courts.

Thus the state school system is much more adaptable to changing conditions and needs than would be the case if state legislatures had less freedom and authority. Most state legislatures meet every two years and school legislation is almost always a very important item of business. Financial programs are adopted for the period of time served by a particular session of the legislature. For example, a legislature meeting biennially will approve a two-year financial program for education.

Such responsiveness to changing conditions could result in a certain degree of instability for the public school systems if state legislatures were complacent or erratic in their decisions. Unfortunately, this seems to be the case at times. However, school systems are adaptable and local support supplements state support. Financing education is considered to be a joint responsibility of the state and the local district. Structural provisions for education are not so rigid that they interfere unduly with educational development. State legislatures are subject to the wishes of the people through methods prescribed for the election of legislators.

It would be difficult to stress too much the importance of the state legislature in public education.

Miscellaneous provisions. As would be expected, there is a variety of references to education in the fifty state constitutions. Some major provisions not previously stated are given below.

Racial discrimination is dealt with in about twenty state constitutions. In five states, there are provisions designed to prevent racial discrimination in the schools. In others, such as those of the southern states, it is required that separate schools be maintained for white and Negro students.

A small number of constitutions state that schools shall be free of sectarian control. Several prohibit religious instruction, and some state that no religious test for admission may be required.

The minimum school term is prescribed in a few cases.

The ages of students for which public schools are free are stated in about twenty constitutions.

A few constitutional enactments are concerned with curriculum matters, such as requiring uniform textbooks throughout the state, prescribing that instruction shall be given only in English and, in one case, mandating free textbooks.

It is interesting to note that current practice now far exceeds these constitutional requirements. As a rule, failure to comply would result in loss of state financial support.

Stability of constitutional provisions. If the vagaries of state legislatures at times impede the proper development of public schools, state constitutions may also do so by prescribing too much stability. Each state constitution provides its own methods of change through a process for the adoption of amendments. In some states new constitutional conventions may be authorized. Both methods of change are difficult to initiate. The Tennessee Constitution is so difficult to amend that in the seventy years of its history not a single amendment has been added.

Constitutions are not so inviolate as their descriptions might indicate. Specific provisions may be ignored if they violate too strongly established beliefs and practices. For example, many state legislatures ignore constitutional provisions requiring reapportionment of their membership at periodic intervals. The constitution of Alabama, adopted in 1901, mandates a reapportionment of the state legislature each ten years. There was no reapportionment until 1962 and it was due to a federal court order.

Specific constitutional provisions which seem perfectly appropriate at the time they are adopted may appear ridiculous at some later period when conditions have changed. The methods prescribed for amending constitutions were originally conceived, no doubt, in recognition of the fact that it would be impossible to write a constitution at a given time adequate for the future. Rather than run the risk of unduly restricting government for some future generation, plans for changing the constitution by amendment were provided. While it has been difficult to change constitutions, this factor has not, in general, seemed to be a major detriment to the progress of education.

Basic Legal Provisions for Education in Local Communities [1]

Local governments are created by a state either through legislative action or constitutional mandate. These governmental units— cities, counties, townships, and other civil districts—are created to serve specific purposes and are endowed by the state with necessary powers to achieve these purposes.

The local government often has been considered the most important level of government with respect to education. There is historical reason for this: the earlier public schools had their authorizations from the local community rather than from the state and the strong tradition of local responsibility for self-government was another important consideration. This philosophy prevails not only in education but in all other areas of local government.

The concept of home rule has been of great significance to education. It has made it possible for the local community to legally and philosophically accept responsibility for the quality of its educational program and to adapt school programs to local conditions and needs. The provision of adequate local authority to achieve these purposes is one of the most significant relationships of government to education.

The extent to which there are basic legal provisions for education in the local community is debatable. Viewed in one way, the local school district, being a creature of its state, is largely independent of other local governments. Court decisions have supported this point of view. In a strict legal sense, these districts have authority to function only as authorized by the state. However, school districts are usually viewed as having the power to carry out the responsibilities delegated to them by the state, whether or not these powers are specifically allocated by the state. The local district can support

---

[1] For a more detailed discussion of the legal aspects of education see other volumes in the Library of Education series.

schools, make curriculum changes, broaden school programs, lengthen the school year, support teacher retirement plans of its own, or take any other action which violates no federal or state constitutional or legislative act.

Municipal governments differ from other local governments, State constitutions or legislative acts often classify muncipal areas according to size for governmental purposes and the types of government possible for each size are usually defined. Cities are governed under charters which in some respects take on the significance of constitutions. These charters are written within the terms outlined by the state and must be approved by the state. Flexibility, therefore, varies from state to state and with size of cities.

City charters usually make provisions for a school system. Within the limitation imposed by the state, these charters may determine the structure of the school system, the functions of the board of education, the functions of the superintendency, and may determine city provisions for financial support. An interesting example of the exercise of this type of leeway is found in the charter of the City of Knoxville, Tennessee. It provides that there must always be a school tax in the city proper of twenty-five cents per one hundred dollars of assessed property valuation above the total local tax levied for support of the county schools in which the City of Knoxville is located.

Summary

The United States Constitution delegates no powers to the federal government concerning education. However, the silence of the Constitution should not be interpreted as lack of interest. On the contrary, the federal government throughout its history has shown a lively interest in education. Although in legal theory states may have had an option in the matter, in a practical sense this was not true because of the importance of education to the people and the accepted philosophy that education is a function of the state. The Congress insisted that territories seeking to become states must make provision in their constitutions for public schools.

Even though no reference to education is made in the Constitution, certain of its provisions have profoundly influenced education. Among these provisions are the general welfare clause, the Tenth

Amendment (implied powers), due process of law, the Fourteenth Amendment, and separation of church and state. In order to determine the relationship of these provisions to schools, court decisions have been necessary. These decisions recognize that education is a function of the states but that states in carrying out this function must do so within provisions of the Federal Constitution. If, for example, educational practice violates the rights of individuals guaranteed by the Constitution, the federal government has power to order changes in such practice and power to enforce these orders. Under the general welfare clause, the Congress may decide to support education in any number of ways. Hence, public education has been influenced strongly by the Federal Constitution but remains a function of the states.

The Supreme Court of the United States has the power to interpret the Constitution and to determine the constitutionality of specific legislative acts. Thus, the influence of the Federal Constitution on education in the final analysis may be determined by court decisions.

State constitutions are the source of the basic legal foundations upon which public education has been developed. Specific provisions for education in state constitutions vary widely from state to state. They do, however, accept responsibility for providing public schools, allocating power and responsibility for establishing and maintaining public schools, and creating needed organization on state and local levels. Some state constitutions contain statements of purposes to be served by the public schools; others merely mandate the establishment and maintenance of public schools. State constitutions in some cases are quite detailed and specific in the definition and allocation of authority and responsibility for public education, while others are general and leave much to the state legislature. The power and responsibility delegated to state legislatures, therefore, varies considerably from state to state. State constitutions contain provisions for financing schools. Additional responsibility for financing education is delegated to the state legislature.

Both federal and state constitutions are sufficiently flexible to make adaptations in the face of changing needs. This flexibility can be achieved through constitutional amendments, the adoption of new state constitutions, or through court interpretations of existing constitutional provisions. Perhaps the greater flexibility has come through court interpretations since they are made, in part at least, within the context of social and cultural factors prevalent when the decisions are rendered.

States have, almost without exception, delegated much of their responsibility for education to local school districts. In the majority of cases, such delegation of responsibility has been achieved by creating school districts which conform to the general provisions outlined in the state constitution or adopted by the legislature. In other cases, municipalities are granted charters by states, either through constitutional or legislative provisions. These charters define the powers delegated to the municipality by the state and are, therefore, the basic legal document for governing municipalities. Such charters usually prescribe the establishment of a school district. A plan for organizing and administering the school district may be set forth. A chief school official and a board of education may be mandated and their powers and duties defined.

Thus, the Federal Constitution, state constitutions and municipal charters affect education in fundamental ways. The metes and bounds of each have never been fully explored, nor have their interrelationships been clarified adequately. In the final analysis, only the courts have power to define the proper sphere of each. While their powers may overlap, they may not be in conflict with each other.

CHAPTER III

Impact of Congress

Since the Federal Constitution makes no reference to education, the doctrine of implied powers leaves Congress free to deal with education as it chooses except in cases where its legislative acts conflict with provisions of the Constitution as interpreted by the Supreme Court. Actually, a federal system of public education seems possible under the Constitution, but the philosophy which came to be generally accepted dictated that responsibility for and control over education should rest with the various states of the Union. This philosophy has served to restrict the role of Congress to that of lending assistance to state school systems except in those instances where it chose to establish and operate its own schools.

Without a constitutional mandate, the will of Congress has been the sole force determining its participation in education. The Congress, being a representative body, presumably reflects the will of the electorate. The support or opposition of the Chief Executive is another force affecting federal participation in education.

Congress has shown a deep interest in education from its earliest days. The nature and character of such interest has varied from time to time depending upon the pressing social, economic, and other issues which affect the country at a given period in history. Congressional interest in education has increased in recent years and has been related in large measure to problems of national security. Since World War II, Congress has devoted considerable attention to proposed legislation affecting schools. Usually, several hundred bills are introduced which relate wholly or in part to education. The Eighty-Fifth Congress, for example, enacted more than eighty laws which in some way dealt with education.

In addition to aiding states and territories in promoting and supporting education, the federal government has traditionally supported and maintained educational programs of its own. A major portion of these programs has been concerned with the national defense. Other phases have involved a multitude of government

22

agencies as well as educational programs and services. A third phase has been the operation and support of programs of education in government territories such as the Indian territories.

Various federal commissions and committees have noted the extensive scope of federal activities in the field of education. The National Advisory Committee on Education appointed by President Hoover reported in 1931 that there was no phase of education that was not a concern of some part of the federal government, and that few people knew how extensively involved the federal government was in educational affairs. A similar committee appointed by President Franklin Roosevelt reported in 1938 that the concern of the federal government in education had increased steadily and that the trend was likely to increase. The report stated further that the needs of the people called for the federal government to extend its responsibilities for the education of children and adults.

In 1948 the Task Force on Public Welfare of the Commission on Organization of the Executive Branch of the Government reported that educational activities constitute a major current responsibility of the federal government. This report listed and briefly described 200 separate federal educational programs and indicated that about $3,700,000,000 of federal monies were appropriated for educational programs in the 1948–49 school year. A report entitled Federal Educational Activities and Educational Issues Before Congress, published in 1952, included information on 298 educational programs operated by various departments and agencies of the national government. Funds set aside for the support of 255 of these programs for the fiscal year of 1950 amounted to over $3,600,-000,000.

The House Committee on Education and Labor reported in 1955 that 315 federal activities in education were supported at a cost of approximately $2,174,000,000. It will be noted that this figure is substantially less than the amount obligated for 1950. The reason for this decline, according to the report, was a reduction in the cost of veterans' education during the period. The cost of other expenditures for education more than doubled during this time.

An examination of this extensive array of educational programs shows that they are diverse in nature and character and that they are diffused throughout the various departments and agencies of the federal government. The national government's interest in education has grown as the amount and character of the education of the people have become of greater significance in the promotion of national welfare, progress, and security.

The purposes of this chapter are to analyze interest in and support of education by the Congress. Major emphasis is on public schools and institutions of higher learning. However, some attention will be given to federally operated and controlled educational institutions. About 200 important laws have been passed by Congress which aid education. The following pages are devoted to the study of a selected number of these laws organized according to major areas of concern and chosen on the basis of their impact on education.

Grants of Land for General Support

The first action by the national government in support of education came in 1785 and thus predates the Constitution. The Continental Congress adopted an ordinance which reserved one section of every township for the support of schools within the township. In 1787, Congress passed the Northwest Ordinance, which included the first statement of policy by Congress with respect to education. The ordinance states that, "Religion, morality, and knowledge being necessary to good government and the happiness of mankind, schools and the means of education shall forever be encouraged." This ordinance did not provide for the reservation of lands to support schools. Perhaps even more important is the principle it enunciated.

The new federal government superseded the initial government under the Articles of Confederation on April 30, 1789. Congress was given power to control and dispose of the national domain in Article IV, Section 3, Paragraph 2, of the Constitution. The first three states admitted to the Union—Vermont, Kentucky, and Tennessee—did not receive public lands for schools since no definite policy of granting such land had been adopted at that time.

A policy was adopted in 1802 in the Ohio Enabling Act which granted the sixteenth section of each township to the inhabitants for schools. A year later, Congress confirmed all previous land grants to schools, gave another township to Ohio for a seminary of learning, and declared that these grants were "for schools and for no other use, intent or purpose whatever." This act vested control of the land in the state legislature.

As other states were carved from the public domain, they too received land grants for schools. Altogether, thirty states received land grants for the support of public schools. The thirteen original colonies and the three states originating from them (Vermont, Maine, and West Virginia), received no land grants for education, nor did Kentucky which was admitted before the policy began, nor Texas which was annexed. No land grants were accorded to the last two states admitted to the Union, Alaska and Hawaii.

It is difficult to assess accurately the impact of these grants on the development of public education in the United States. But it goes without saying that they firmly identify the government's concern for education and its realization of the importance of public schools. Although abuses occurred in the handling of these lands and the income from them, the lands, in general, served the purposes of providing initial support for local schools and encouraging states and local communities to provide for the education of their children. Returns from these lands furnished the basis of state systems of school finance.

The use of income from these grants was unrestricted as long as it went for the support of public schools, and the states and local communities had complete freedom to determine the types of schools to be created and the nature of the programs and services which would be offered. The granting of lands is the only example of general assistance to education by Congress. All other aid has been for specific purposes.

Establishment and Maintenance of Schools

Some educational goals sought by the federal government have been pursued through the establishment, support, and control of special schools. Chief among such goals has been the securing of our national defense. Five institutions have been established for this purpose.

The first school established to promote the national defense is the United States Military Academy. It was created in 1802 by an act of Congress. The purposes of the academy are to develop officers for the Army and to provide a foundation for the continued development of personnel for careers in this branch of service.

Four years of instruction are offered in the academy which is located at West Point, New York. Graduates receive the degree of Bachelor of Science. As would be expected, the curriculum leans heavily toward those subjects deemed most useful in preparing young men for military careers, subjects such as mathematics, the sciences, engineering, and physical fitness.

The number of students authorized for the academy is at present approximately 2500. Appointments are made on both non-competitive and competitive bases and are made by members of Congress and certain other government officials. Fairly high scholastic and physical standards for admission are required of all appointees. Cadets are selected from the territories and possessions of the United States as well as from every state in the Union.

The United States Naval Academy was established in 1845. Its primary function is to prepare career officers for service in the Navy. The academy is located at Annapolis, Maryland, and is supervised by the Bureau of Naval Personnel of the Navy Department. The academy enrolls approximately 3600 men per year. Students are selected in the same manner that appointments are made to the military academy. Graduates receive the Bachelor of Science degree. A limited number of foreign students are admitted to the academy.

The United States Coast Guard Academy was established at New London, Connecticut, in 1910. The academy prepares young men for careers as commissioned officers in the United States Coast Guard. While the curriculum includes liberal arts subjects, it leans heavily to subjects in marine engineering and the sciences. When the course of study is completed successfully, a Bachelor of Science degree is awarded. Appointments to the academy are not made on the basis of state quotas although most states are represented in the enrollment. Enrollment numbers about 600.

The Merchant Marine Academy, located at Kings Point, New York, was founded in 1942. Its purpose is to prepare young men to serve as officers in the United States Merchant Marine Fleet. Enrollment is approximately 900. Students are selected on a quota basis from the various states by appointment and/or competitive examination. A four-year curriculum is offered which leads to the degree of Bachelor of Science.

The newest of the military academies is the United States Air Force Academy located at Colorado Springs, Colorado. It opened at Lowery Air Force Base at Denver in 1954. The academy was authorized for the purpose of preparing officers to serve in the United States Air Force. Students are carefully selected and must meet exacting physical and mental entrance requirements. Maximum enrollment is approximately 2500 students. United States male citizens between the ages of seventeen and twenty-two years are eligible for appointment to the academy. Graduates receive the Bachelor of Science degree.

In addition to the five undergraduate institutions named and briefly described above, the Department of Defense operates the Industrial College of the Armed Forces, the National War College, the Department of Defense Military Assistance Institute, the Armed Forces Institute, and the Armed Forces Staff College. The general purpose of these institutions is to enhance national security by specialized training of selected leadership in those fields which are deemed to serve best the national defense. Most of the educational offerings are on the graduate level.

There are numerous other educational institutions and agencies under government control and support which are designed to promote the national defense. Public colleges and universities, and even high schools, are sometimes centers for preparation in the military sciences, with support from the federal government. The land-grant institutions are well known for their military programs.

The Congress established in 1857 the Columbia Institution for the Deaf. It is located in the District of Columbia. The name was later changed to Gallaudet College and, in 1864, it was authorized to grant degrees in the liberal arts and sciences. The Eighty-Third Congress defined its status as a college and its relationship to the federal government. Its functions are to provide education and training for deaf persons and to further the education of the deaf in other ways. The college operates an elementary and a secondary school for deaf pupils in the District of Columbia and surrounding territory. These schools serve as laboratories for the preparation of teachers of the deaf.

Howard University, located in the District of Columbia, is a semi-public institution under a self-perpetuating board of trustees. It was established in 1867. The federal government appropriates substantial sums for the current operation of Howard University, the amount in recent years ranging from four to five and one-half million dollars annually.

The Congress has established and supports schools for Indians in the Indian territories and supports and maintains public schools in its other territories. In addition, the government provides for the education of children of military personnel in establishments maintained by the armed forces at various points on the globe.

Land-Grant Colleges and Universities

In addition to granting public lands for the establishment and maintenance of schools in local communities, support was extended to higher education with the passage of the Morrill Act in 1862. This act granted to each state 30,000 acres of public land for each of its congressional members to be used in the support of a college which would have as its primary purpose teaching "such branches of learning as are related to agriculture and the mechanic arts . . ." In those states where sufficient public lands were not available, their equivalent in value was given each state in the form of script.

Buildings, building sites, and further appropriations needed to carry on programs of the land-grant institutions were to be provided by the state legislatures. Thus, the Congress defined a specific set of purposes to be served by the institutions and granted financial support to encourage states in the establishment and further support of such institutions. Proceeds from the sale of the grants of land to each state were to become a perpetual fund, with the income used to support the land-grant institutions.

A second Morrill Act was passed in 1890. It provided for a direct annual appropriation to each state or territory of $15,000 to be increased at the rate of $1,000 per year until the total annual appropriation was $25,000, to be used in support of the land-grant institutions. The total annual appropriation was increased to $50,000 per year by the Nelson Amendment to the Land-Grant College Act in 1905, which provided for an annual increase of $5,000 until the $50,000 per year figure was reached. The Bankhead-Jones Act of 1935 and its amendments adopted in 1952 increased further the appropriation to land-grant colleges and universities.

A second extension of the land-grant college and university movement occurred in 1887 when Congress passed the Hatch Act which appropriated money for the establishment of agricultural experiment stations. Acts passed in 1906 and 1925 increased the annual appropriation to each state for this purpose to $90,000. Additional federal support has been available, usually on some matching basis. Specific appropriations for agricultural research at the experiment stations are made through the Hatch Act of 1955, as amended. Essentially, this act consolidated previous related programs which had been authorized initially by separate legislation. Legislation establishing the experiment stations makes clear the intent of Congress to improve agricultural production, marketing, distribution, and utilization through research and experimentation.

The functions and services of land-grant colleges and universities were substantially extended by the Smith-Lever Act of 1914. The Department of Agriculture, the land-grant colleges and universities, and county governments cooperate in supporting county extension agents and their staffs in most of the counties in the nation. Extension workers provide instruction to farmers, farm wives, and rural youths for improving agricultural production and farm life.

Congress thus made possible the development of a new type of institution of higher learning with emphasis placed on the agricultural and mechanical arts. Major purposes to be served were in the realm of the practical arts through which people seek economic self-sufficiency. This movement emphasized a utilitarian value of higher education which had been largely lacking in the past. A new concept of higher education was created by emphasizing research to contribute original knowledge and extension to bring this knowledge to the potential consumer as an additional service of an institution of higher learning. This concept has been of perhaps greater interest to foreign countries than any other phase of American education and has been more widely emulated than any other.

Vocational Education

A concept of educational purpose similar in philosophy to that of the land-grant college and university underlies the support of vocational education by the federal government. Congress passed the Smith-Hughes Act in 1917 which authorized the allocation and distribution of federal funds for vocational education in secondary schools. The purpose of this program is to provide youth with the knowledge, skills, abilities, and working habits needed to achieve success in business, industry, labor, and commerce.

The act also provided for vocational preparation in the fields of agriculture, home economics, trades and industries, and the preparation of teachers of these subjects. Funds were allocated on a matching basis and in proportion to the ratio of certain segments of the population of the state to corresponding segments of the population of the entire country. Funds were used to pay salaries of teachers and supervisors in the public schools, administrative officials in state departments of education, and teacher preparation personnel in institutions of higher learning.

In order to participate in the Smith-Hughes program, a state was required to secure legislative approval of the provisions of the act, to designate the state treasurer as custodian of federal funds, and to set up a state board for vocational education. Furthermore, the state board was required to submit to the Office of Education plans for vocational education showing how federal, state, and local funds were to be spent. The state board was also required to prepare and submit an annual report showing how the funds were actually expended.

In 1936, the George-Dean Act extended the Smith-Hughes Act to include education for distributive occupations.

The George-Barden Act of 1946 extended vocational education to include additional appropriations and support for vocational education in the fishery trades and distributive occupations. This act also provided an appropriation to extend and improve practical nurse training and similar training in other health occupations. Additional amendments now provide for area vocational education programs to train technicians needed for national defense. This addition is part of the National Defense Education Act of 1958.

Under these provisions, vocational instruction is available to young persons through the regular day schools, to out-of-school youth and adults who are in need of occupational training, and to any other person who can profit from the instruction by virtue of the occupation he is following or plans to follow. Some idea of the magnitude of the vocational education program below the collegiate level is indicated by the fact that in the school year of 1957–58, 3,629,339 persons were enrolled in the various classes offered through this program. Three-quarters of a million were in agricultural education, 1,500,000 in home economics, nearly 1,000,000 in trades and industries, nearly 300,000 in distributive education, and 27,000 in practical nurses training.

In 1920, the Smith-Bankhead Act initiated a policy of cooperation between federal and state agencies in providing education for the handicapped in order that such persons might achieve vocational independence.

School Building Construction and Current Operation

The Lanham Act, passed in 1941, allocated the first federal money specifically for construction, operation, and maintenance of school buildings, although federal funds had been used for school building construction under the National Industrial Recovery Act of 1933. Various activities of the government, many of them involving national defense, have brought about important changes in the composition and character of local communities. The primary impact of these changes on the public schools were increases in enrollment and retirement from the tax rolls of substantial local property for taxation purposes. Because of the school finance problems thus created, compensatory funds were made available by the federal government to the affected school districts.

The demand for assistance in meeting educational needs of areas affected by the war continued after World War II ended. Federal assistance for this purpose has been extended by successive acts since that time. A study was made by a subcommittee of the House Committee on Education and Labor in 1949 to determine what legislation, if any, was needed to assist local school districts with housing problems brought on by federal activity. In 1950, as a result of this study, public laws 815 and 874 were enacted. These acts place responsibility for providing financial assistance to local school districts affected by federal installations with the United States Office of Education.

More than 4500 school districts have been allocated funds under these two acts since 1950. Between 1950 and 1960, the amount disbursed for capital outlay was $759,251,000. The amount appropriated for current expenses of schools in affected school districts between 1950 and 1960 was nearly 955 million dollars.

Thus, substantial federal appropriations for both building construction and current operation have gone to school districts in areas affected by federal installations. Strong efforts have been made to extend the principle of federal support for these purposes to all public schools in all states. Thus far, no such measure has been able to clear both Houses of Congress.

Education of War Veterans

The federal government has provided educational programs to rehabilitate service-disabled veterans of World War II and the Korean Conflict, to restore local educational opportunities due to active military service in World War II and in the Korean War, and to educate war orphans. Congress has appropriated the funds it deemed necessary and has charged the Veterans Administration with responsibility for administering and supervising the programs.

Each of these programs makes use of established educational institutions or industrial establishments and each is administered through regional offices of the Veterans Administration. Veterans may continue their education in institutions of higher learning, public schools, business establishments, or on a farm in combination with formal study. Education for war orphans must be in vocational schools or collegiate institutions.

Payments are made to the individuals to cover the costs of their education. The readjustment education program for World War II veterans also included provisions for payment to the institution in which the veteran was enrolled. World War II veterans who availed themselves of the opportunity of continuing their education at government expense totaled 7,800,000. Many thousands of these veterans, who otherwise would never have had such opportunities, completed college and university programs. About 2,275,000 veterans of the Korean War furthered their education at government expense. Many of these veterans were also able to complete a college education. More than 13,000 war orphans had enrolled in school under provisions of the Veterans Administration program by the end of 1959. In all cases, veterans were free to choose their own programs of study, but were advised through counseling services supplied by the Veterans Administration.

Vocational Rehabilitation and Education Services

A program was established by Congress in 1920 to develop cooperative support between the federal government and the states for the rehabilitation of disabled persons. This service is designed to develop the ability of disabled persons to do useful work. Federal funds are distributed for technical and professional assistance to persons in need of rehabilitation, to support research and demonstration projects, and to provide instruction to disabled persons for the purpose of helping them become employable.

The program was expanded by the Barton-LaFollete Act of 1943. This act states that half the cost of services such as transportation, medical examinations, surgery, hospitalization, the purchase of needed appliances and occupational tools, and training and maintenance must be paid by federal funds.

The vocational rehabilitation program was further strengthened in 1954 with the passage of additional amendments designed to further stimulate the development of vocational rehabilitation services. The financial structure of the program was again improved and the scope of services broadened.

Equipment and Other Property

Federal aid to education has been made available through an extended program of distributing either free or, in many cases, at nominal costs substantial amounts of property accumulated by the government for military purposes but which either became obsolete before its use, or when the need for its use became obsolete. Congress passed an act following World War I in 1919 authorizing the Secretary of War to sell to public schools, universities, and other educational institutions upon application in writing "such machine tools as are suitable for their use which are now owned by the United States of America and are under the control of the War

Department and are not needed for government purposes" at 15 per cent of their original costs.

The Surplus Property Act passed in 1944 set up a more systematic procedure for giving away the huge stockpiles of property which were no longer needed for defense and for making the property available to educational institutions, health institutions, and civil defense organizations. At the conclusion of the Korean War, Congress greatly increased the amount of available surplus property for donation to public health and educational institutions in an effort to clear government inventories of obsolete equipment, supplies, and properties.

Federal personal property cannot be offered for sale to the general public until it has been made available for donation to non-profit, tax-exempt school systems, institutions of higher learning, or health institutions. Surplus personal property can be donated to serve purposes of civil defense.

Items are classified as surplus when they become obsolete or are in over-supply. Most of the items which would normally be obtained by public health and educational institutions have been available to these institutions in some measure through the surplus property donation program. About 90 per cent of such property has originated in the Defense Department. New technical developments hasten the obsolescence of government property and dictate frequent replacements. Hence, federal property is likely to continue to be available for educational purposes. The value of such property given away in a single year has exceeded $300,000,000 more than once.

Surplus real property has also been made available to educational institutions on either a lease or sale basis. Frequently, sale prices are substantially less than replacement costs. On some occasions, installations of considerable size have been turned over to educational institutions for conversion to their purposes. Between 1949 and 1959, a total of 20,353 acres of land and 8494 buildings were turned over to educational institutions by the federal government. The market value of these properties was judged to be $33,733,000, in contrast to their costs of $108,192,000 to the government.

School Lunch

The National School Lunch Act was adopted by the Seventy-Ninth Congress in 1946. Its purpose was:

> . . . To safeguard the health and well-being of the Nation's children and to encourage the domestic consumption of nutritious agricultural commodities and other food by assisting the states through grants-in-aid and other means in providing an adequate supply of foods and other facilities for the establishment, maintenance, operation, and expansion of non-profit school lunch programs.

The 1946 act consolidated several previous enactments beginning with one in 1935 which provided for an annual appropriation to the Secretary of Agriculture equal to 30 per cent of the gross receipts from duties collected under custom laws to be used for a number of purposes, one being,

> . . . To encourage the domestic consumption of such commodities or products by diverting them by the payment of benefits or indemnities or by other means, from the normal channels of trade or commerce or by increasing their utilization through benefits, indemnities, or by other means, among persons in low income groups.

Under the School Lunch Act, funds are apportioned to each state to be used for school lunch services. The amount allocated to each state is determined by the number of children from five to seventeen years of age in the state and variations in per capita income of the respective states.

This program was supplemented by the Agricultural Act of 1954 designed to increase the consumption of fluid milk. It provides for reimbursement to non-profit elementary and secondary schools for milk purchases. The Department of Agriculture establishes the maximum amounts that may be paid to participating schools and child-care institutions under this program. Payments are on the basis of four cents for each half-pint of milk served in excess of the first half-pint in a Type A lunch and three cents per lunch for lunches of other types.

The school lunch program and the special milk program are administered by the state departments of education. The total value of such assistance during the decade of the fifties was more than two billion dollars.

International Education

Advances in communication and transportation have rendered obsolete former patterns of international relationships. Due to the need thus created, a new federal educational program originated in 1946 with the passage of the Fulbright Act. This act provided for the establishment of a system of credits based on the sale by the United States of surplus property abroad, the credits to be used for international education exchanges. Two years later, the Smith-Mundt Act set up a broad program of international education through exchange programs. The purpose of the exchange programs is to promote mutual understanding and confidence between the United States and other countries. This is attempted through acquainting other people with American objectives and policies.

The International Cooperation Administration was established in the Department of State in 1955. It has responsibility for coordinating foreign assistance programs and for the conduct of the several mutual security programs. Necessary funds come from federal sources and from foreign cooperating countries. Foreign countries request a desired program and usually contribute about two-thirds of the cost.

Technical assistance in developing the economy of cooperating countries is thought to be one of the best ways of building a stronger free world. Heavy reliance is placed upon education for the development of both human and natural resources. Programs have been developed in agriculture, industry, public administration, and health services.

The latest agency in this area of education is the Peace Corps, established by an act of Congress in 1961. Its purpose is to supply technicians and teachers from the United States to assist underdeveloped nations.

Libraries

Although this type of federal aid has never been specified for the public schools, it is nevertheless important inasmuch as it is further evidence of the continuous interest of the federal government in agencies and institutions which contribute to general education. The first appropriation for books made by Congress took place in 1800.

This appropriation provided the nucleus of the Library of Congress.

The Library of Congress was authorized initially as an aid to Congress. This is still a major function. As the Library has developed, however, its services have been extended to all branches of the government and to the general public.

Among its services is the provision for reading materials for the blind. These materials are provided on loan, without charge, to blind persons and to institutions serving blind persons. They are made available through the thirty regional circulating libraries located in large cities of the United States.

More than 50,000 legally blind individuals utilize these services. In 1950, the Library of Congress had 4986 titles in braille, 400 titles in moon type, and 3639 titles in talking books. It also had available record-playing machines.

In 1956 Congress passed a Rural Library Act designed to encourage and assist states in extending library services to rural areas which were either without a library or which had inadequate library services. The act provided for an annual appropriation of $7,500,-000 for five years to be used for grants to states in extending and improving rural library programs. Allocated funds were to be matched by the respective states on the basis of their rural population and per capita income. The act was extended for another five years in 1960.

On the basis of this program, some states are making incentive grants to counties and sub-regions within the states to help develop cooperative library services to bring books to rural people. Other states are supplying bookmobile services to new areas or developing new branch libraries in sparsely settled rural communities.

Special Subjects and Selected Phases of School Programs

Cultural developments within the last two decades as well as international tensions have created new concern for the adequacy of public education. The National Science Foundation Act of 1950 and the National Defense Education Act of 1958 are only two of the acts which reflect this concern.

National Science Foundation Act. This act was created "to promote the progress of science; advance the national health, prosperity, and welfare; secure the national defense and for other purposes." The Foundation has developed an extensive program in science education as a part of its activities.

The science education emphasis includes institutes for science and mathematics teachers, fellowships for graduate study in the sciences and mathematics, projects to improve course content in science and mathematics, special projects in science and mathematics education, training through the use of research grants, and international science education projects.

There are three types of science and mathematics institutes; the summer institute, the academic year institute, and the in-service institute. During the summer of 1960, 411 summer institutes were offered for teachers. There were 33 academic year institutes in the 1960–61 school year. In-service institutes numbered 191 for the same year, with an additional 13 experimental in-service institute programs for elementary school personnel.

Since its inception, the summer institute has served over 53,000 teachers. The academic year institutes have provided a full year of study for over 5000 high school teachers and 75 college teachers. The in-service institutes have served approximately 21,000 high school teachers and 750 elementary school teachers. The major purpose of these institutes is to improve the competence of science and mathematics teachers in their subject matter fields.

The several other phases of the science education and mathematics education emphasis, while less spectacular, have nevertheless served to improve mathematics and science teaching in the public schools.

The National Defense Education Act. An explicit statement of the relationship of education to the national defense as viewed by Congress is set forth in the National Defense Education Act of 1958. It states:

> . . . the security of the Nation requires the fullest development of the mental resources and technical skills of its young men and women. The present emergency demands that additional and more adequate educational opportunities be made available. The defense of this Nation depends upon the mastery of modern techniques developed from complex scientific principles. It depends as well upon the discovery and development of new principles, new techniques, and new knowledge . . .
>
> To meet the present educational emergency requires additional

effort at all levels of government. It is, therefore, the purpose of this act to provide substantial assistance in various forms to individuals, and to states and their subdivisions, in order to insure trained manpower of sufficient quality and quantity to meet the national defense needs of the United States.

The act contains ten titles, each designating a particular kind of support for education (except Title I which deals with general provisions of the Act). Funds in the amount of one billion dollars for grants and loans were made available for four years to be used at all levels of education, both public and private. All titles are administered in the Office of Education except Title IX which pertains to the establishment of a Science Information Service. It is administered by the National Science Foundation. Title VIII is administered by the Vocational Education Program, which is within the Vocational Education Division of the Office of Education. It makes provisions for area vocational education programs of less than college grade for the training of skilled technicians needed in the national defense.

Title VI and Title V(b) extend the teacher preparation institute concept first set forth in the National Science Foundation program to guidance and foreign languages. Provision is also made in Title VI for language research, modern foreign language fellowships, and centers for foreign language and cultural subjects.

Title V(a) makes financial assistance available to the states to support testing programs for students in secondary schools, to identify those with outstanding abilities and aptitudes, to support programs of guidance and counseling in the public schools for the purpose of advising students concerning courses best suited to their abilities and aptitudes, and to encourage such students to continue their educaton through and beyond the high school.

One of the unique features of the NDEA program is Title II which makes available loan funds to colleges and universities for qualified and needy students to continue their education beyond the secondary school. Recipients of such loans are encouraged to become teachers by reducing the sum which has to be repaid by 10 per cent for each year taught after graduation up to a maximum of five years.

Title IV provides fellowships for students who wish to become college teachers. These programs extend through the doctoral level.

Title X is designed to assist state departments of education in improving their statistical services. Grants may be made to states in amounts of up to $50,000 per year for this purpose.

Title III makes assistance available to elementary and secondary schools for improving the teaching of science, mathematics, and modern foreign languages. Funds may be used for the purchase of laboratory or other needed equipment and for minor remodeling of laboratories and other space used for science and mathematics teaching. States are allocated funds for expanding and improving supervisory and other services to public elementary and secondary schools in these areas of instruction. Funds under this title must be matched by the states on a dollar-for-dollar basis. Loans are also permissible to private schools for improving instruction in science and mathematics.

Another feature of the National Defense Education Act is Title VII which provides grants to foster research and experimentation in the educational uses of mass media of communication. Proposals are received by the Office of Education for projects in research concerned with the newer educational media and designed to improve the educational programs of schools through use of these media. Extensive assistance is provided under Title VII for disseminating information concerning the proper utilization of these media.

Exceptional Children

Provisions for educational services to the blind by the Library of Congress, the Vocational Rehabilitation Program and education of disabled veterans show the long-term interest of the federal government in educating the the handicapped. A further expression of this interest was passage by Congress of the Fogarty-McGovern Act in 1958 which makes available federal grants for the training of teachers of the mentally retarded. In 1961, Congress provided funds for the preparation of teachers of deaf children and for hiring speech typologists and audiologists.

During the year ending June 30, 1962, one million dollars was made available in the program to train teachers for the mentally retarded, $1,575,000 for training teachers of the deaf, and $250,000 for preparing speech typologists and audiologists.

Cooperative Research Program

A further venture of the federal government in education was begun under the terms of Public Law 531 as passed by the Eighty-Third Congress. This act empowered the United States Commissioner of Education to "enter into contracts for jointly financed cooperative arrangements with universities and colleges and state educational agencies for the conduct of research, surveys, and demonstrations in the field of education."

Researchers are invited to submit proposals to the Office of Education on any phase of education which they feel should be studied. A wide range of subjects have been covered in projects which have been approved. Among these are projects on curriculum design, child development, education of the retarded, education of the able, learning theories, teaching methods, and test development.

The general aims of the Cooperative Research Program are to stimulate the development of new knowledge regarding educational problems and to encourage the application of knowledge to the solution of these problems.

During the first four years of the program, 273 research projects were approved and $9,200,000 was appropriated to carry them out.

Summary

The Congress has been largely free to express its interest in and support of education within the confines of the public will and in accordance with the accepted concept that education is a function of the several states. It has shown continuous and abiding concern for public education since its earliest days, and has expressed this concern through a wide variety of acts supporting education. In general, such aid has been of two kinds; supporting the state school systems through grants for specific purposes, and through the establishment of government schools and educational agencies. The early land grants to the states for the establishment and maintenance of public schools were for general purposes. Without exception, subsequent enactments have been for specific purposes with the provision of financial or other support.

The range of support covers public education from the elementary school through college and university levels, with increasing emphasis on graduate study. Special support has centered on agriculture and mechanical arts education, vocational education, education of the handicapped, and in recent years, education of the gifted. Monies have been provided for scholarships and loans to students, and for grants to veterans of World War II and the Korean War, as well as grants for the preparation of elementary, secondary, and college teachers, and grants for the improvement of content in teaching areas. In addition, financial support has been provided for research in education, for school house construction and maintenance in federally-impacted areas, for the operation of schools in these areas, for educational equipment and supplies through the surplus property acts.

The array of government education agencies and programs is without overall administration, planning, or coordination. Neither is there a clearly defined policy of support to state school systems. There is no overall administration or coordination of these areas of support.

Newer government concern for education emphasizes its quality and the areas of learning considered most essential to the national defense. Hence, programs of assistance in counseling and guidance, education of the gifted, and programs in the sciences, mathematics, and foreign languages have been adopted. The relationship of national security to the quality of education and its dispersion among the people are notable outcomes of international tensions created by the struggle between democracy and communism.

A second notable new development in the efforts of Congress to promote education centers on developing international understandings. The extensive exchange study program and technical assistance programs to underdeveloped countries are examples of this effort.

A further more recent expression of government efforts to further education is found in the provision of funds for research in education and emphasis on preparing more specialists with outstanding abilities in science, mathematics, and foreign languages.

CHAPTER IV

Role of State Legislatures

Under the doctrine of education as a state function, it has been necessary for each state to develop a system through which responsibility for and control over schools can be exercised. State constitutions accept responsibility for providing schools and allocate authority to do so largely to the legislative branch of government. The state legislature, therefore, has great power over the public schools, although it may delegate much of it to designated sources. Thus, legislation is a more potent influence on education than state constitutions.

As was noted in Chapter II, the legislative branch of a state government is frequently required by the state constitution to establish and maintain common schools. This general allocation of power leaves the state legislature with much flexibility and freedom of action with respect to public education. In other instances, state constitutions specifically define a plan for organizing and administering the public schools, list officials needed, and outline their powers and duties.

State legislatures must act in terms of constitutional provisions pertaining to or related to education. Provisions of state constitutions cannot be contrary to those of the Federal Constitution. Legislative action must fall within the limitations set forth in both federal and state constitutions. The doctrine of implied powers is operative on the state level as well as on the federal level, resulting in greater freedom of choice in courses of action open to the legislature. Constitutional limitations to state power over schools do not always lie in specific references to education but rather in provisions which deal with rights and privileges of the citizens.

State legislation is more easily accomplished than constitutional change. Hence, placing a large measure of responsibility for control over education in the hands of state legislatures makes possible quicker action and greater responsiveness to the public will. Most state law-making bodies meet biennially. Matters concerning the public schools are usually of main importance in deliberations of these bodies. Their responsiveness to changing conditions and needs is an important factor in maintaining and operating a satisfactory state school system.

As is to be expected, there is a great range in the degree to which state law-making bodies exercise their powers over education. This range is related to such factors as constitutional provisions, interest of the law-making body in schools, the extent to which the people desire good schools, patterns of local control in education, and the leadership which is in power. It is not surprising, therefore, to find a vast array of state legislation on education which covers a wide variety of subjects ranging from the simple to the complex.

There is an even greater variety of legislation than constitutional provisions. A review of all such legislation would be a mammoth task and not within the province of this volume. As is true of state constitutional provisions for education, however, there is much that is similar among the states in legislation for education. This chapter analyzes the scope and nature of legislative action concerning education by major subject areas. The fact that what is a legislative prerogative in one state is a constitutional mandate in another makes this task a more difficult one.

Organization and Administration

As indicated above, one of the essential tasks of government is organizing and administering education. All states have created at least minimum machinery on the state level for these purposes. Some states have chosen to retain much authority and control at the state level, while others have delegated much authority and responsibility to local school districts. There are, however, certain common provisions among the states. The responsibility of the state in the actual administration of schools is discharged through the state board of education, the state department of education, and the chief state school officer.

State board of education. Provision is made for state boards of education in all states, about half being mandated by the constitution and the others being created by the state law-making body. Powers and duties of these boards vary greatly. With the exception of Illinois, Michigan, North Dakota, and Wisconsin, states have boards of education with general responsibilities for the public, elementary, and secondary schools.

Except for these four states, the state board is the policy-making body for the state public school system. Among other responsibilities and powers generally exercised to some degree by state boards of education are:

1. Setting forth ways and means of carrying out adopted policies;
2. Maintaining general control over the schools;
3. Determining the curriculum;
4. Providing minimum standards;
5. Developing and adopting necessary means for enforcing and carrying out state law pertaining to education.

State boards vary in number of members from three in Mississippi to twenty-three in Ohio, with seven members the number in twelve states. Eight states have fewer than seven members and seven states have more than eleven members on their boards of education. The general trend seems to be toward somewhat larger boards.

There are three common methods of selecting state board members—election, appointment, and ex officio membership by virtue of position held. Seven states have board members composed entirely of elected individuals and one state has an ex officio board. The entire membership of the boards of seventeen states are appointed (as a rule by the governor, but in some instances by official bodies) while eight states have no appointed board members.

Some qualifications for board membership are set forth in most of the states, although these are very minimal qualifications. No state sets forth educational attainment as a prerequisite for board membership, but studies show that approximately seven out of eight board members have attended college. Some of the stipulations for membership include the following:

1. One member to be selected from each congressional district;
2. No more than a stipulated number shall belong to the same political party;
3. Persons representing textbook companies are not eligible for membership;
4. Members shall hold no other state office;
5. One or more members are to be chosen from persons engaged in educational work.

Terms of office vary from three to nine years, except in New York where the term is thirteen years. As a rule, a majority change of membership is prevented by staggered terms of office. Ex officio members serve for the term of office they hold. It is customary for members to serve without pay although a few states provide small honorariums for each day of attendance at meetings or each day spent on business of the board. In addition, travel and subsistence costs for attendance at meetings is supplied. Boards meet, as a rule, a specified number of times during the year and such additional times as the business of the board may require.

The discussion above relates to those state boards of education which have general responsibilities for the public school system. There are in addition about 300 state boards in the 50 states which have responsibilities for various aspects of state educational programs. Among such are those with responsibilities for:

1. Vocational education (although in the great majority of states the vocational education board is also the general state board of education);
2. Teacher education;
3. Education of the handicapped child;
4. Administration of school building programs;
5. Teacher certification;
6. Library services;
7. Some aspects of higher education.[1]

State board responsibilities for higher education are so diverse that it is extremely difficult to draw significant valid generalizations. In some instances, the general state board of education also serves as the board for state colleges. In other instances, special state boards are created for each public institution of higher learning or a single board serves all the state institutions. Some states have separate boards for vocational and trade schools, schools for the handicapped, and other special schools.

The chief state school officer. Each state has provided for a chief administrative officer of the public school system, either by constitutional provision or statutory enactment. A majority of states use the title *Superintendent of Public Instruction,* or a similar title.

---

[1] Calvin Grieder, Truman M. Pierce, and William Everett Rosenstengel, *Public School Administration,* 2nd ed. (New York: The Ronald Press Company, 1961), pp. 39–45.

The title *State Commissioner of Education* is becoming increasingly popular.

In general, the chief state school officer serves as the executive officer of the state board of education and the chief administrative officer of the state department of education. He is charged with overall supervision of the public schools, the organization and functioning of the state department of education in accordance with established policy, preparation of curriculum guides and courses of study, the collection, analysis, and interpretation of educational statistics, enforcement of minimum standards, the issuance of teacher certificates, approval of school building plans, preparation of budgets, submission of reports to other governmental bodies, the distribution of state funds in accordance with laws and policies, and approval of standards for teacher preparation.

In many cases, the chief state school officer also has the power to interpret school laws and to decide controversies appealed to him from local boards of education. An increasing function of the chief state school officer is to serve as spokesman for the public schools in matters concerned with school objectives, achievement of educational aims, and educational needs. It is clear from the above that the chief executive officer of the public school system has much responsibility.

Qualifications for the office have, in general, fallen below the exacting requirements of the office as its powers and duties have increased. Age and place of residence are the most common legal qualifications. Some level of educational attainment is specified in the law of about half the states; however, these requirements are frequently so general that they mean little. It is still possible in a few states for a person to serve as chief state school officer who cannot qualify for the lowest grade of teacher certificate issued by the state.

The term of office varies from one year to six years. A four-year term is the most common, being the requirement in twenty-three states in 1960. Some states do not permit the chief state school officer to succeed himself, while in others indefinite tenure is possible.

In twenty-four states the chief state school officer is elected by the people. Appointment by the state board is the method of selection used in twenty-four states. In the other two states the officer is appointed by the governor.[2]

Importance of the position of chief state school officer is being recognized to an increased degree by both the profession and the general public. A growing trend emphasizes his responsibility for providing leadership in the continuous development and evaluation of the state school system. The nature of the political environment in which the state superintendency exists in some states makes difficult this demanding role.

The state department of education. All state school systems have a state department of education. This agency is responsible for state level operation of the state school system. It carries out functions allocated to it by the state legislature, the state board of education and, in some cases, the state constitution. The state board of education develops policies and the state department of education is charged with their implementation. The chief state school officer is a member of the staff of the department of education and its administrative officer.

Major functions of state departments of education, according to the National Council of Chief State School Officers, are leadership, regulation, and operation. States vary greatly in the degree of emphasis placed on each of these functions. Some state departments of education, as in New York and North Carolina, exercise much more control than do their counterparts in other states, Michigan and South Dakota, for example.

The leadership role is increasing in importance and reflects a definite trend away from former major emphasis on accounting, reporting, and inspection. Various aspects of leadership often stressed are overall coordination of the state school system, planning for further development of the system, research, consultative services, public relations, and evaluation. However, regulatory functions are not to be minimized. They include meeting reasonable standards for curricula and programs of instruction, protecting the lives, safety, and health of children, the prudential management and economical use of school funds, and efficiency in managing the educational enterprise.

More and more concern has been shown in recent years for the

---

[2] Grieder, Pierce, and Rosenstengel, *op. cit.,* pp. 45–51.

operational principles employed by state departments of education. Involved in this are the leadership function itself and the methods employed in providing leadership. The trend is toward a consulting and helping relationship to local schools rather than the authoritarian approach inherent when primary emphasis is on control and direction. The goal of much leadership from state department today is to assist in the development of leadership and initiative within the school districts. Another concern for operational functions involves the freedom of state boards of education to serve as policy-making bodies and evaluating agencies rather than as supervisors concerned with the specifics of operation and management.

The increasing importance of state departments of education is also reflected in the size of staffs. In the early days of state departments of education, a superintendent and a limited number of clerks constituted the typical staff. Today, more than 6000 professional persons are employed as members of the staffs of the fifty state departments of education. The secretarial, clerical, and other employees total another 6000. Some state departments are still very limited in size, with six states having from ten to twenty members in their departments. There are two states whose staffs number more than 600 persons. Professional staff members in the various state departments range from two to thirty per 1000 teachers in the public schools of the states.

Qualifications of professional personnel in state departments have often been at a lower level than the quality of service demanded, largely because of low salaries (as compared to salaries paid in the better school systems for administrative and supervisory personnel). Civil service regulations govern the appointment of state department of education personnel in some states. The chief state school officer makes recommendations for appointments which are subject to approval by the state board of education.

State departments of education are generally organized according to areas of service. As many as thirty-three areas of service are offered by four or more state departments of education. However, patterns of organization vary to such a degree that it is very difficult to draw appropriate generalizations. All departments are not organized according to areas of service. The pattern most generally favored by authorities provides that the state board of education serve as the chief policy agency for the public schools and that its chief executive officer serve as the state superintendent of education.

The local school district. The local school district has been defined as an instrument for assisting the state in carrying out its educational functions. A local school district consists of a geographical area, often coterminous with some other local unit of government, within which a board of education representing the citizens has responsibility for the public schools in the district. Such districts are given specific grants of power by the state, frequently including the power to levy taxes for school purposes. Requirements set forth in the state constitution or by statutory enactment usually leave considerable freedom to the school districts, varying greatly from state to state. States retain final authority over education, however, and the local school districts have only such powers as are granted by the states or as implied in carrying out assigned functions. Permissive laws often allow considerable discretion to the local boards of education. The localizing of responsibility for education has made the public schools of this country unique in many respects.

The school district is generally viewed as a quasi corporation rather than a municipal corporation. The distinction is sometimes difficult to draw, the major difference being that the quasi corporation is regarded as an agency created to carry out state functions rather than local functions.

Local districts are of several types—independent elementary school districts, independent high school districts, township districts, county districts, and city districts. The school districts vary greatly in size from those which include a single elementary school with one teacher and perhaps only a dozen students to the New York City School District which has an enrollment of more than 1,000,000 pupils. The trend is toward larger school districts which include elementary and secondary schools and sometimes junior or community colleges.

Local school districts of more than one school are divided into school attendance areas, each served by a single school. Some attendance areas overlap others; for example, a high school attendance area may include several elementary attendance areas.

The local board of education. School districts must have some kind of structure through which local schools may be organized and administered. All states through constitutional or statutory enactments have created boards of education for this purpose. Such boards are composed of lay citizens who reside in the school district. In the great majority of cases they are elected by popular vote of the citizens. Thus, local control of schools is vested in a lay board representing the entire district.

The nature of powers and duties of local boards of education often corresponds to those of the state board of education for the state school system. The board is the responsible agency for establishing and operating the local public schools. Some states allocate responsibility for junior or community college education, adult education, and various special education programs to the local board of education.

Determining and adopting policies under which the local schools are administered is the chief function of the district board of education. Selection of a superintendent of schools is another important function, except where some other method of selection prevails. The local board of education appoints all personnel employed in the school system, in most cases upon recommendation of the superintendent. Approval of the school budget and, in many cases, adopting provisions for financing the schools is also a local board function. Another very important role of the board is the continuous evaluation of local school programs. These functions are served in varying degrees by boards of education, depending upon the freedom under which they operate, the personnel who constitute board membership, and the caliber of the superintendent.

A function of some local boards of education which has been much debated is the levying of taxes to finance the school budget. Fiscal independence is traditional with boards of education in New York State and some other parts of the country. Other boards are sometimes given the power to tax within limits placed by the state, often by constitutional amendments. Fiscal independence gives the board power to provide the school program it believes best for the district.

Local boards of education vary in size from three members to fifteen or more in a few instances. Authorities generally agree that five to seven members constitute the board of ideal size. It is estimated that 95 per cent of all local school board members are elected by popular vote. Election for membership, in some districts, must fall on dates other than those of party primaries. Provision is made for appointment of board members in six states; in thirty-five states all boards are elected by popular vote, while in nine states most boards are elected but some are appointed. Appointments may be made by mayors, city councils, county courts, and state legislatures. In most cases, school boards are nonpartisan in composition.

The term of office for approximately 99 per cent of all board members ranges from two to six years with the trend toward a longer term of office. It is customary for membership to be staggered so that some continuity of membership will be preserved. It is not unusual for members to enjoy long tenure of office.

The local school superintendent. The school superintendent serves the local school district as the administrative head of the local schools and the executive officer of the board of education. The superintendency is more than a hundred years old. The legal basis for the position is less clear than that of the school district or the school board. Some state constitutions and legislative acts make no references to it at all while others enumerate the powers and duties of the office in great detail. The position is found in all states, however, and it is mentioned in about forty-four state school codes. Employment of a superintendent is not usually mandated by state law but is authorized. Legally, the superintendent of schools is an employee of the board, and not an officer of the board, even though frequent references are made to his function as the executive officer of the school board. While the law does not give him this status, practice does.

A chief function of the school superintendent was mentioned earlier, serving as executive officer of the board of education. Other duties include:

1. The selection and recommendation to the board of all employed personnel;
2. Preparing the budget;
3. Administering the budget;
4. Determining building, curriculum, personnel, and other needs of the schools;
5. Recommending courses of action to the board;
6. Serving as a community leader in the study and improvement of the local schools;
7. Evaluating the school program and planning for its improvement.

Clearly, if all these functions are to be served, the school superintendency is a demanding position. Those aspiring to the position should be individuals of considerable ability who have had advanced preparation in the field of educational administration.

A great weight of professional judgment supports appointment of the superintendent by the board of education. Actual practice corresponds to this point of view in the vast majority of cases. In some states, the county superintendent is appointed by the county board of education. In some county school districts in Tennessee, for example, the superintendent is appointed by the county court. In a few states, however, superintendents of county school districts are elected by popular vote either in all or part of the county districts. The term of office ranges from two to six years with current trends pointing toward a term of four or five years. The position of the school superintendent is more tenuous than that of any other professional educator. Where boards appoint the superintendent, they can also dismiss him. About half of the states provide no tenure or continuing contracts for superintendents.

The intermediate school district. The intermediate district exists on the level between local districts and the state. This unit includes an area composed of two or more local school districts, and it provides services to the local districts. Such units developed in the days when school districts generally were very small and when some agency was needed to perform services which the districts were too small to perform economically for themselves. Initial need appeared to center on enforcing state regulations, gathering statistics on schools for the state, and supervising the distribution of state funds. Since the district is also a subdivision of the state, it serves to assist the state in carrying out its educational functions.

Some kind of intermediate district is found in thirty-four states. The other states have only local districts, except Hawaii which has a single board of education under which all schools in the state are governed. In some states, the intermediate districts correspond to the counties. The county will then be subdivided into local districts. In some states the intermediate unit has no board of education, while in others provision is made for such a board. In all instances, such districts have a superintendent.

The functions of the intermediate district appear to be changing with the current trend emphasizing the provision of professional services to the local districts within the unit. The former assignment of enforcement of regulations is minimized and leadership for school improvement is stressed.

Financial Support

States have always assumed responsibility for financial support of schools. At one time, most of the support for schools came from the state. This trend has been reestablished in the last few years. Much of the early state school monies came from income derived from the land grants to states for establishing and maintaining public schools.

As these funds served to stimulate local taxes for education, the per cent of total support from the state gradually declined until state taxes for schools began to appear about 1840. Since early in the twentieth century, a variety of state taxes for schools have been adopted. Sources of state school support are income from the permanent endowments established largely from the land grants (slightly more than 1 per cent of the state revenue for schools), state taxes earmarked for school purposes, and state appropriations for education from the general fund. Sales, income, severance, and license taxes are the major sources of state support for schools.

The tax base for school support by states is being broadened by reliance upon new sources of revenue. There is less reliance by the state on property taxes for schools, more dependence upon general funds, and less tendency to earmark taxes for educational purposes. The property tax is generally being accepted as a proper source of local school support. The total amount of state aid to school districts was $4,560,855,000 in the 1957–58 school year. The range in per cent of state support for public elementary and secondary schools in this year was from a low of 7 per cent in Nebraska to a high of 94 per cent in Delaware. The median support was 35 per cent.[3]

Determining an equitable plan for the distribution of state funds to the various school districts has posed difficult problems. Two critical questions have been involved in the search for a suitable formula: how can educational need be measured, and, how can local ability to support schools be measured? The latter question is

---

[3] Albert R. Munse, Eugene P. McLoone, and Clayton D. Hutchins, *Public School Finance Programs of the United States, 1957–58* (Washington, D.C.: Office of Education, 1961).

based on the assumption that the state will not take over complete responsibility for financing schools but will operate on a partnership basis with local districts.

Earlier, plans of distribution such as those based on the school census, enrollment or attendance ignored both these questions and, in effect, tended to distribute funds without regard to where they could do the most good. Gradually, the concept developed of utilizing state funds to equalize educational opportunity among the various districts in the state. Implementation of this concept demanded serious efforts to ascertain educational need as well as ability to support schools in the various local districts within the state.

These two questions recognize that school districts vary widely. The two most important criteria of variability are, of course, need within the district for education and ability of the district to pay for the education needed. Factors associated with both of these questions are numerous and some are very difficult to objectify. In order to measure need the states have taken into account such factors as the school population, sparsity of population, and differences in the proportion of pupils enrolled in school programs which vary in unit cost. More intangible factors such as the relationship of the general cultural level of the community to educational needs have not been included in the measurement of need.

The measurement of taxpaying ability, although difficult, has been achieved through the development of economic indexes and other measures. As sources of income of the people have increased, property has become a less satisfactory measure of community wealth and, therefore, taxpaying ability. Consequently, indexes of economic ability usually include items such as the following: volume of sales taxes; number of passenger car licenses purchased; personal income taxes paid (federal); some measure of consumer purchasing power; assessed valuation of property; value of farm products; value added by manufacture; payrolls; and value of minerals produced. The particular factors to be selected in a given state are dependent upon the sources of wealth and income in the state. Data on from five to seven of these economic indexes are used as a rule to derive a formula for determining the amount of state aid which goes to each district and the amount of revenue each local district must raise in order to qualify for the state aid. The state's portion comes from the sources of revenue identified while the local district usually raises its portion of the school funds from local property taxes.

The discussion above tends to oversimplify the problem of equitably allocating state monies to the support of education in local communities. After much experience in distributing state aid by flat grants and special purpose grants, the concept of a foundation program has gradually emerged and is now accepted in principle by nearly all of the states, although many of these states still support to a limited degree some of the earlier plans in addition to the foundation approach.

The core of the foundation concept is the equality of educational opportunity. States attempt to tax wealth for educational purposes where it exists and to support the education of children wherever they live. In short, the foundation program seeks to provide a minimum level of educational opportunity for all children in the state, a floor below which no district should be permitted to fall. Satisfactory measures of need and ability are basic to the success of the foundation program. There has been a strong tendency in some states for local districts to view the minimum program as also the maximum program. Recent trends show an increase in support from the local district.

Development of the foundation program was a monumental step in school finance. Characteristics of a satisfactory foundation program include providing essential, reasonably adequate, and well-rounded educational opportunities for all who should benefit from public education, a bona fide state-local partnership plan for financing this foundation program of educational opportunity, and the same minimum local effort toward financing the foundation program by each district. The state should supply to each district, on an objective basis, the difference between the funds available from the required uniform minimum tax effort and the cost of the foundation program. The plan for financing the foundation program should assure reasonable equity for all taxpayers. Provisions of the program should encourage sound and efficient organization, administration, and operation of local districts and schools. The plan should provide maximum opportunity and encouragement for the development and exercise of local leadership and responsibility in education; the citizens of each local school system should be authorized to provide and finance such educational opportunity beyond the foundation program as they desire; the foundation program should be cooperatively developed by representative citizens who have a genuine interest and concern about public education; and the program and procedures should emphasize continuous evaluation and sound long-range planning.[4]

It will be noted that these factors make possible a productive state-local partnership in financing the schools. Earlier experience with foundation programs which tended to minimize local initiative by placing the burden of school support on the state are offset by such factors.

Some reference to how capital outlay funds are provided is essential. The state has been slow to accept responsibility for financing the cost of school plants and historically, therefore, this has been the responsibility of the local district. However, emergency needs created by installations of the federal government during and following World War II led to assistance from the national government for schoolhouse construction in affected school districts. There is now a trend toward state participation in financing new school buildings. The local unit, however, still supplies most capital expenditures. Foundation programs in some states are beginning to include support for capital outlay. State bond issues are another method of raising funds for school building construction. (Most local support for buildings and other capital outlay comes from bond issues.) Limits on the amount of bonds a district can levy are usually defined by the state. As a rule, the limitation is expressed in terms of a percentage of the assessed value of property in the school district.

Any discussion of state school support would be incomplete without reference to higher education. State institutions of higher learning have no local sources of support except charges to students, income from contracts for services, admission fees to athletic games, and the like. Therefore, state responsibility for financing higher education is of a different order to that of financing public schools. The tremendous increase in the demands for higher education and the growing complexity and scope of programs and services make problems of state support increasingly difficult to solve. There is less objectivity in methods of allocating state funds to institutions

---

[4] Roe L. Johns and Edgar L. Morphet, *Financing the Public Schools* (Englewood Cliffs, N.J.: Prentice-Hall, Inc., 1960), pp. 268–70.

of higher learning than there is to school districts. Studies in determining need for higher education and costs of the various programs in higher education are greatly needed. Capital outlay expenditures for state institutions of higher learning must come from the state or from self-amortizing loans, such as those available through the federal government for construction purposes. It appears inevitable that an increasing proportion of the state budget for education will go to colleges and universities and other institutions beyond the high school level.

The School Curriculum

The power to decide what is to be taught in the public schools, at what level it is to be taught, the period of time it is to be taught, and even the method of teaching lies with the state. However, in general, states have not used this power to set up prescriptions in detail, although all states have passed some legislation pertaining to required subjects to be taught in the public schools. This power is often delegated in part to the local school district acting through its board of education and superintendent. Control over the school curriculum often rests in large measure with the state board of education. The state department of education then becomes responsible for carrying out decisions and regulations of the state board.

Responsibilty for carrying out state statutes dealing with the curriculum is also assigned to the state department of education. These laws often define a rather specific program of studies for the elementary schools, specifying subjects to be taught and the grade levels at which they are to be taught. In other states, laws are passed authorizing state boards of education to adopt stipulated program provisions. Less specific definition of curricula for the high school grades is common, although particular subjects are required at this level also. However, more elective subjects are permissible. Requirements usually include American history, English, mathematics, and science. Staffs of state departments of education consider their major responsibilities in curriculum to extend beyond the regulatory and enforcement levels to leadership in improving the quality of work offered in all areas of learning. Hence, curriculum specialists have an important place on staffs of state departments of education. Many state departments of education view the production of curriculum materials as one of their responsibilities. Such materials may include general courses of study, curriculum guides, and the production of special teaching materials. Staffs sometimes start by drafting tentative materials to be considered by local teachers; at other times, discussions with groups of teachers are initiated to establish interest and need. Frequently, the department personnel work with local teachers in the actual development of curriculum materials.

There is growing concern for state department responsibility in evaluating more adequately the effectiveness of curriculum materials. This calls for research and experimentation which most staffs are not prepared to conduct. Present emphasis on statewide testing programs may have some beneficial effect on the curriculum, if test results are related to pupil growth and curriculum needs. A more systematic determination of student needs to be met by curriculum requirements is desirable.

Textbooks are the major source of curriculum materials in most states. Therefore, the responsibility for selecting textbooks is a very important one. The states handle this matter in a number of ways. About half permit the local school authorities to adopt textbooks with no prescription or control from the state or any intermediate body. The next most common authority for the adoption of textbooks is the state board of education; twelve states employ this method, and seven states place authority for textbook selection in the hands of state textbook commissions or committees. In the remaining states, a list of textbooks is approved by the state board of education or a textbook commission composed of local school authorities who choose the textbooks to be used for each subject. Multiple adoptions of textbooks are made in thirteen states and in five other states multiple adoptions are offered in some subjects.

Textbooks are usually adopted for periods of four to six years, although some are adopted for shorter and/or longer periods of time. The state board of education or the state department of education determines the period of an adoption in sixteen states and the state legislature in ten states. The relationship of courses of study to textbooks is important. Where legislation requires that particular subjects be taught for stipulated purposes, a criterion for selecting textbooks is available.

The state department sometimes chooses to provide teaching

materials in certain subjects rather than depend on a textbook. Such materials usually deal with the effects of alcohol, tobacco, and narcotics. State courses of study are influenced by the organization of content in textbooks in most states, while in twelve states the reverse is true. There seems to be an increase in the interest of states in establishing a more obvious relationship between textbooks and courses of study. This would seem to be a particular need in those states which select textbooks for statewide use.[5]

Minimum Standards

States have shown interest in both the scope and quality of available education. A prevalent method of influencing quality is the stipulation of standards to be observed which are often necessary for the accreditation of a school. National and regional educational agencies also concern themselves with standards of accreditation. Frequently, states work in conjunction with these agencies although they have their separate programs.

The usual practice is for state standards to be determined by the state board of education or by the state legislature, or both. In either event, the state department of education is customarily the agency responsible for enforcing these standards. A common approach to enforcement is the incorporation of standards in the minimum program which must be met before the local school district participates in the distribution of state funds. Standards usually are concerned with such factors as health, safety, lighting, heating, sanitation, buildings, transportation, equipment, libraries, laboratories, maps, globes, textbooks, the curriculum offered, the preparation of teachers, teacher-pupil ratios, teacher loads, class size, and length of school year.

While state accreditation is most often concerned with the secondary schools, there is an increase in the exercise of state responsibility in the accreditation of institutions of higher learning and elementary schools.

Earlier emphasis on quantitative standards is giving way to consideration of criteria which deal more directly with the quality of

---

[5] Howard H. Cummings and Helen K. Mackintosh, *Curriculum Responsibilities of State Departments of Education,* U.S. Department of Health, Education, and Welfare (Washington, D.C.: Office of Education, 1960), pp. 20–26.

instruction. More and more efforts center on using standards for accreditation as means for the continuous improvement of schools rather than as an authority with which to force improvement. This is consistent with current state department of education philosophy that the major role of the state department lies in the exercise of leadership functions to assist local school districts in continuous educational development. Former uniformity encouraged by insistence on merely meeting quantitative standards is giving way to developing diversity in local school systems and directed toward more adequately meeting the educational needs present in the system.

Teacher Certification

The power to decide whether or not a person is qualified to teach is extremely important. This power resides with the state and each of the states has established its own standards for certification, no two of which are the same. The number of types of certificates issued by states ranges from one to fifty-seven. Conventional requirements, although by no means universal among the states, include citizenship, an oath of allegiance, recommendation from a teacher training institution or employing official, a general health certificate, completion of a special course in the history or geography of the state, and a minimum age.

As yet, no adequate scientific basis exists for determining eligibility for certificates. Two major objective factors relating to professional competence are employed: the number of years of college work completed in designated curricula, and the number of years of actual teaching experience. Neither effectively discriminates between the competent teacher and the less able teacher.

Certification standards have been raised gradually during recent years. However, the two major classifications remain, standard and substandard certificates. The standard certificate is based on meeting the requirements set forth by state regulations for preparation to teach in the position for which the certificate is issued. A substandard certificate may be issued under certain conditions to those who have not met the requirements for the standard certificate. All states still issue the substandard certificate. It is usually issued for one year, but it can be renewed if certain professional requirements have been met during the year such as earning a stipulated amount of college credit. This certificate is issued only in cases where persons who meet the requirements for a standard certificate are not available. According to the Research Division of the National Education Association, 6 per cent of the teachers in the United States held substandard certificates in 1956.

Although there are various types of standard certificates, the probationary and continuing certificates are the most common. The former is usually granted to new teachers upon completion of an undergraduate college program and is good for a specified number of years, usually three to five years. It may be renewed in most states by showing evidence of successful teaching experience and/or the completion of additional preparation. In some cases, the certificate cannot be renewed but the person can qualify for a higher ranking certificate. The continuing certificate is issued for a stated period, most often one year beyond that required for the probationary certificate. It may be valid for six to ten years and is usually renewable upon presentation of evidence of successful experience and additional training.

The power to issue certificates is usually vested in the state department of education. Six states have authorized city boards of education to issue certificates for teachers hired by the city, while four other states have given state colleges the authority to issue certificates.

Important trends in teacher certification are a reduction in the number of types of certificates issued, more precise definition of requirements for eligibility, the elimination of life certificates, and the establishment of higher educational requirements.[6]

Teacher Education

The teacher certification function obviously gives the state great power over the nature and scope of teacher preparation programs. Influence is not limited to the prescription of requirements which an applicant must meet in order to be properly certified. Legislative provisions, state board of education policies, services of state departments of education, and advisory groups on the state level all influence teacher education.

---

[6] Chester W. Harris, ed., *Encyclopedia of Educational Research* (New York: The Macmillan Company, 1960), pp. 1354–55.

No clearcut pattern for the administration of institutions of higher learning which prepare teachers has been developed. A 1955 study stated that the state board of education was the governing body of public teacher training institutions in fourteen states, a separate single board governed such institutions in nine states, in ten states each teachers college had a separate governing board, and in fifteen states all public institutions of higher learning were governed by a separate board for higher education distinct from the state board of education.[7]

Most of the states now approve institutions for teacher preparation. The vast majority of these states vest the power of approval in the state department of education. Basis for approval by the states range all the way from limited and general information on the nature of the preparation programs to detailed analyses of preparation programs evaluated by the application of specific criteria.

Divisions of teacher education and certification have been established in several state departments of education. The functions of such divisions is to enforce regulations concerning teacher preparation; approve teacher preparation programs, provide professional services for upgrading teacher education, and to certify teachers. There is a trend toward the establishment of such divisions in other states.

A steady growth in recent years of state level advisory councils and committees on teacher education has occurred. Such councils and committees usually function under state department auspices. Members of these groups represent the colleges and universities which prepare teachers, public school groups, the state education association, and the state department of education. Their general function is to study teacher education needs and to propose improvement measures.

No widely accepted single pattern of teacher preparation has been developed. There are, however, three major phases in a teacher education curriculum which are generally accepted, although the specifics of each vary considerably from institution to institution and state to state. These three areas are: general education emphasizing subjects which contribute to the overall cultural develop-

---

[7] Fred F. Beach and Robert F. Will, *The State and Education,* U.S. Department of Health, Education, and Welfare, Misc. No. 23 (Washington, D.C.: Office of Education, 1955), 175 pp.

ment of the student; specialization in the teaching areas for which the student expects to seek certification; and professional education which includes educational psychology, educational philosophy, curriculum development, teaching methodology, student teaching, and evaluation of learning. The general trend is toward longer periods of preparation with considerable discussion beginning to appear on the merits of a five-year teacher preparation program.[8] More emphasis is being placed on preparation in the subject matter specialization, the continuous education of teachers, and the payment of teachers for advanced levels of training only if the teacher is in the field of specialization in which he has had preparation.

Teacher Welfare

States have generally assumed the responsibility of protecting the teacher against unjust loss of position, and providing appropriate sick leave and retirement programs. There is little uniformity among the states with respect to practice in these areas.[9]

Two kinds of tenure laws have been developed; one provides for permanent tenure after a period of probationary service, and the other is a continuing contract which requires the board of education to notify a teacher by a specified time should his services not be desired for the coming year. There is still considerable difference of opinion over the merits of such legislation.

The first statewide system of teacher retirement was adopted by New Jersey in 1896. All states had some type of retirement plan by 1957, except South Dakota. In addition, local retirement systems are found in a number of the larger cities.

Although retirement systems differ in many respects, there are some areas of similarity. Retirement systems tend to serve all employees of the school system and in some cases the state system is the general retirement plan for all state employees. The systems are financed by the state establishing a reserve fund in order to honor payments when they are due. The state and the employee then pay an equal amount into the retirement plan each month, usually a

[8] Harris, ed., *Encyclopedia of Educational Research*, pp. 1452–81.

[9] For a detailed discussion of teacher welfare see Leslie Kindred and Prince Woodward, *Staff Welfare Practices in the Public Schools*, Library of Education series (Washington, D.C.: The Center for Applied Research in Education, Inc., 1963).

percentage of the salary of the employee. The total amount is used to provide an annuity which can be used when retirement occurs, the amount of payment being determined on the basis of actuarial studies. Another type requires payment into the system of an amount sufficient to buy a fixed allowance at retirement. The contribution rate would then depend on the fixed amount desired.

The formula most commonly used to determine retirement payments is based upon years of service and the income earned during this period of service; the longer the period of service, the greater the retirement income. Retirement systems also tend to grant death benefits to the employee's beneficiary or to his estate. Most plans contain a provision for refunding to the member the amount of his contribution plus interest, if a request is made by the applicant. The age of sixty is the most common age for eligibility to retire voluntarily. A definite period of service, usually thirty or thirty-five years, is also a basis for eligibility to retire. Mandatory retirement in some systems is at seventy, in others sixty-seven, and still others, sixty-five.

Many states permit a member of the retirement system who has become disabled to qualify for benefits if he has been in service from ten to fifteen years. As a rule, the same method is used for determining the amount of the allowance that is used in computing regular retirement payments. Special consideration for members permanently disabled is included in some retirement plans, usually by allowing a specified percentage of the member's payments had he continued working until the retirement age.

Retirement systems have been improved in recent years by increasing the retirement benefits and by placing the systems on a more sound actuarial basis. Recently, retirement provisions for teachers in some states have been substantially improved by teachers qualifying for social security.

Sick leave policies and the provision of substitute teachers may be left to the jurisdiction of local school districts or provisions may be made in state minimum foundation programs. The typical sick leave plan allows a stipulated number of days per year of leave with pay. If the allowable number of days is not used, they may be accumulated to a stated number. The school system accepts the responsibility for employing substitute teachers in case of a permanent teacher's absence. Most systems keep a list of eligible substitute teachers.

Welfare provisions are an important contribution to educational effectiveness. They tend to make the teaching profession more attractive and they protect teachers from worries relating to unfair loss of position or loss of income because of illness. They also furnish assurance that the retirement years will not be without compensation.

Nonpublic Schools

No consideration of the education of American citizens is complete without reference to the nonpublic schools. During the past thirty years, enrollments in colleges and universities has been divided almost equally between private institutions and public institutions with the trend toward a higher proportion entering public institutions, particularly since World War II. Enrollment in nonpublic elementary and secondary schools has increased steadily in percentages of the total number enrolled in all schools in the last half-century. The Office of Education estimates that if present trends continue, by 1965 the nonpublic elementary and secondary enrollment will be in the ratio of one to six for all children in elementary and secondary schools in the United States. Schools which carry such a sizeable percentage of the educational load are naturally of interest to state governments.

States are free to control nonpublic schools just as they control public schools unless provisions and interpretation of the constitutions are to the contrary. Since the majority of state laws pertaining to education apply to public schools, laws have been passed to assure that nonpublic schools meet the same minimum standards as those adopted for the public schools.

Institutions of higher education which confer degrees usually must seek incorporation in the state where they are located. An instrument of incorporation is viewed as a contract and, therefore, the state cannot violate provisions of the act. Charters of incorporation may limit educational institutions to serving the purposes stated in the charter; they may prevent institutions from owning real property in excess of a fixed amount, and they may deny freedom to confer degrees unless stipulated conditions are met. Acts of incorporation are rarely required of institutions which do not grant degrees.

Approval is required by some states for the establishment and operation of certain types of nonpublic schools. Such official approval may be required of nonpublic schools that are incorporated as well as those that are unincorporated. Legislatures in some states delegate to the state department of education power to work with nonpublic schools that voluntarily submit to state supervision. Such schools may be called accredited schools or recognized schools. Many nonpublic schools seek approval in order that their programs may be officially recognized and their graduates afforded the same consideration as public school graduates where matters of licensing are involved. For example, private teacher preparation institutions seek official approval in order that their graduates may be certificated under the same conditions as graduates from the approved public institutions.

Since legislation concerning compulsory attendance usually requires that the school attended provide at least the minimum educational program which the state defines as satisfactory, approval of the educational program of a nonpublic school is essential if its students are to meet compulsory attendance regulations. If the nonpublic school does not comply with such standards, the state may not accept attendance of children as meeting the compulsory attendance requirements. This regulation is enforced in a number of states.

Where state legislation makes public funds and services available to nonpublic schools, approval of the nonpublic school is usually a prerequisite to participating in the distribution of funds. A few states make public funds available to private institutions without setting forth the purposes for which the support is to be used. In these cases, private institutions ordinarily submit a request for funds to the legislature. It is customary for institutions receiving such aid to be inspected by the state department of education and to make reports to this agency concerning the use of the aid which was granted. State legislation which permits appropriation of public funds to nonpublic schools usually provides for support of scholarships or tuition, textbooks, health and welfare services, transportation, the school lunch program, and payment for instruction.

All of the states grant tax exemption to certain nonpublic schools.

Responsibility for the administration of such exemptions is vested in public agencies. These agencies satisfy themselves that the criteria are met under which tax exemptions are permitted. In a small number of states, teachers in nonpublic schools below the collegiate level must receive state certificates.[10]

Miscellaneous Powers and Provisions

The range of legislative attention to education in the states of the Union is so great that any attempt at categorization must necessarily leave out many specific acts which are of interest and, in many cases, of considerable importance. Indication of this range may be inferred from the preceding pages, even within the categories listed. Some legislation which falls outside these categories is discussed below.

Laws requiring school attendance up to a given age or until completion of a stipulated grade are now universal. However, the specific requirements of these laws vary considerably.

States often adopt laws to prevent the establishment of certain types of business, such as saloons, within a stated distance of a school building.

Legislation concerning the schools varies in character and scope as social and cultural conditions change. For example, in time of war, interest in the teaching of patriotism increases and this may be reflected in legislation. Following wars, general concern may shift to the education of veterans. Some states gave attention to this problem shortly after World War II and after the Korean War.

The rise of communism seemed to initially stimulate the passage of legislation to keep the schools from teaching communism. Current emphasis appears to have shifted in some cases to legislative requirements that the evils of communism be taught in the public schools.

Occasionally, a legislature may be concerned about the content of one or more textbooks. Legislative investigations of textbooks and the teaching in some subjects is not without precedent. A classic example of legislation to prevent teaching a presumed evil occurred

---

10 Fred F. Beach and Robert F. Will, *The State and Nonpublic Schools,* U.S. Department of Health, Education, and Welfare (Washington, D.C.: Office of Education, 1958), 152 pp.

in the famed Tennessee statute outlawing the teaching of the theory of evolution.

While states have always been interested in higher education, the legislation devoted to this subject has increased tremendously in recent years. In 1961, 2393 legislative proposals relating to higher education were introduced in state legislatures. Seventeen hundred and eleven of these were enacted into law and the remaining 682 were rejected.[11]

While not a legislative function, the power of eminent domain is granted by states to school systems.

Summary

State legislatures acting on the concept that education is a function of the state have always been concerned with education. Legislation adopted which affects schools is of great scope and variety. The increasing importance of education to individual and national welfare is reflected in current trends in state school legislation. It is possible to classify much of this legislation into major areas of concern. These areas are briefly summarized below.

An early subject of state legislation and one which has persisted throughout our history is concerned with adequate provisions for organizing and administering the public schools. States typically discharge this responsibility by the creation and maintaining of state boards of education, state departments of education, chief state school officers, and local school districts. The power to organize and administer local schools within legal limits is entrusted to these local districts. As a result, considerable control of education has remained in the hands of people in communities served by the schools. Intermediate districts have been created in a number of states to provide services to the primary districts.

Legislation in the field of higher education has assumed increasing importance in recent years. Such legislation includes the establishment of institutions of higher learning, provisions for their organization and administration, provisions for certain types of state control, and provisions for financial support. In general, the

---

11 S. V. Martorana and Ernest V. Hollis, *Survey of State Legislation Relating to Higher Education,* U.S. Department of Health, Education, and Welfare (Washington, D.C.: Office of Education, 1962).

structure of higher education is relatively independent of the structure of the public schools.

A second major responsibility assumed by the state is providing financial support for the public schools. When the support provided by interest on endowments from federal land grants to the state for establishing and maintaining schools proved inadequate, state taxes were added. State support has increased rapidly in the last half century and a variety of taxes have been levied to supply the necessary funds. Taxes earmarked for education appear to be on the decline while reliance upon general funds is increasing. Scientific measurement of educational need and the ability to pay as a basis for the equitable distribution of state funds to school districts has occupied a great deal of attention. Problems still remain in these areas. Development of the minimum foundation program which seeks to establish a floor of educational opportunity for all is one of the notable advances in school finance during the past several decades.

States exercise the right to determine what is taught in the public schools and at what grade levels it is taught. The selection of textbooks and other teaching materials frequently accompany the exercise of this power.

In keeping with the concept of equal educational opportunities, states, as a rule, accept the responsibility of establishing and maintaining standards of school excellence which are to be met by all school districts. The allocation of state funds is often related to meeting such standards.

The certification of teachers is a state function. Requirements for certification are established either by legislation or state board action, or both. The state department of education or some other state agency is authorized to grant certificates. Adequate means of determining fitness to teach have not been fully developed. Reliance at present is largely on measures of formal preparation and experience in teaching.

Stability and status of the teaching profession have been enhanced by the establishment of teacher welfare provisions which include tenure laws, retirement plans, sick leave, and provisions for substitutes. Disability allowances are permissible under some retirement plans.

Nonpublic school enrollments are considerable in this country.

The extensive responsibility nonpublic schools accept for educating the citizenry justifies state concern for their effectiveness. Theoretically, states have power over these institutions except as may be contrary to federal and state constitutional provisions. In practice, regulation of nonpublic institutions tends to follow the standards established for public schools in the respective states. The provision of state funds in some cases for the support of nonpublic schools in such areas as transportation, textbooks, operation, health services, as well as the importance of meeting compulsory school attendance requirements justify regulation from the state level in order to assure the minimum educational opportunity the state defines as acceptable.

All states exempt property of these schools from taxation.

Much legislation which cannot be classified in the areas listed above has been passed by the states. It tends toward the specific and often is in response to conditions and pressures unique to a particular generation.

It should be emphasized that state legislation in all of the areas discussed above is lacking in uniformity. While a few of the topics listed may be the subject of legislation by all states, in the majority of cases this is not true. Even in a subject of interest to all states, like compulsory attendance, the specifics of legislation will vary considerably from state to state. This is a normal expectation inasmuch as the various states have much autonomy in the decisions they make concerning the public schools.

Teacher education is becoming increasingly important to the respective states. All of the states exercise considerable control over teacher education through such means as approving the teacher education curricula of institutions of higher learning, controlling the administrative boards of the institutions, appropriating funds for teacher education, establishing and maintaining advisory and consultory services in the field of teacher education, and in the prescription of certification requirements.

Current trends indicate a continuation of the extensive attention states give to education. Size of state budgets and the proportion of state revenues devoted to the public schools account for only a part of this extensive activity. The constant pressure for more and better educational programs is the major reason.

CHAPTER V

Federal and State Courts

A major function of the judicial branch of government is to determine the constitutionality of legislative acts. Another function is to determine the extent to which performance complies, or does not comply, with the law. Whether or not a law or a performance meets constitutional requirements is determined only when a specific case is brought before the court for decision. The courts have no authority to initiate action. All legislative acts are considered to be constitutional until ruled otherwise.

Constitutional provisions at both federal and state levels are often necessarily couched in broad, general terms which serve only the purpose of general policy. Desirable flexibility in law-making is thus possible, enabling legislatures to take into account changing conditions and needs. Such freedom creates many opportunities for differences of opinion on what is or is not constitutional. Even persons trained in the law sometimes disagree on the constitutionality of an act.

Changing social and economic conditions, changes in what people view to be important, and new knowledge open new fields for legislation. Efforts to adapt education to changing needs and demands, therefore, is reflected in school legislation. As a result, questions arise from time to time which only the courts can answer.

The role of the courts in education is far from the passive one which may be implied from the above. Despite the lack of authority to act on their own initiative, the nature of cases brought before the courts and the character of decisions rendered have profoundly affected schools. While the courts seek to rule on the intent of a law and the relationship of this intent to permissibility under the Constitution, judges have considerable leeway in making their interpretations. A court whose judges tend to be conservative may render a decision that a more liberal court may later nullify by a contrary decision on a similar issue. The reverse is also true, of course. While this merely emphasizes the fact that judges are human, it has caused criticism of the courts. However, no one has suggested that the initial decision on an issue is necessarily the better one because of its seniority.

The problems and issues which the courts are called upon to decide vary with the cultural pressures and issues of a given age. Judges cannot and should not be unaffected by the needs of the generation they are serving. Constitutions and legislatures are man-made and they exist to serve man. The American system of government has proven itself to be adaptable to the changing needs of its people. The courts have contributed to this adaptability through the character of their decisions. A rigid and inflexible interpretation of the Constitution without reference to the cultural context in which questions arose would have had the opposite effect on our national development. Since decisions are usually made on the basis of a choice of interpretations, the social philosophy held by the judges is important.

Selected court cases on both federal and state levels are presented in the following pages and an interpretation of their impact on education is offered.

The Federal Courts

Decisions of the Supreme Court are considered in this section. Cases appearing before the Supreme Court are often appealed from lower courts, and many originate in state courts. Supreme Court decisions are usually of crucial importance and affect the entire nation.

Article III, Section 2, of the Constitution defines the jurisdiction of the federal courts in these words:

> The judicial Power shall extend to all Cases, in Law and Equity, arising under this Constitution, the Laws of the United States, and Treaties made, or which shall be made, under their Authority; . . . to Controversies to which the United States shall be a Party; . . . between Citizens of different States, . . . between Citizens of the same State claiming Lands under Grants of different States, and between a State, or the Citizens thereof . . .

Inasmuch as education is not mentioned in the Constitution, it can come before the Court in an indirect fashion only. Supreme Court cases affecting education have arisen under the First and Fifth Amendments which deal with civil rights, the Fourteenth

Amendment which is concerned with protection of all citizens under the law, the general welfare clause, and cases involving the powers and functions of the states or the federal government.

The Supreme Court has expressed reluctance to deal with cases which concern educational policies adopted by states. One of the justices once voiced fears that the Supreme Court might become a national board of education. Nevertheless, decisions affecting education have been made consistently where a provision of the Federal Constitution was at issue.

Cases reaching the Supreme Court which affect education have steadily increased in number since the beginning of the twentieth century. If only cases considered to be of major importance are included, nine occurred before the beginning of the twentieth century, nine during the first quarter of the century, and more than thirty such cases have been heard since 1925.

These major decisions have been classified under the following headings:

1. Cases Involving Rights of Parents and Students;
2. Cases Concerned with the Rights of Teachers;
3. Cases Concerned with Rights of Races in Schools;
4. Cases Concerned with the Powers of School Authorities;
5. Cases Concerned with the Rights of Nonpublic Schools.[1]

Decisions may be also classified according to the constitutional provisions under which they were tried. The decisions reported below fall into three general categories.

Clarification of federal and state powers and functions. Eight major cases have reached the Supreme Court which involve state and federal authority and responsibility affecting education. The basic question in each case was whether or not a state could exercise a specified responsibility or power over education without violating the Federal Constitution.

The first is the famous Dartmouth College Charter Case.[2] A charter was granted by the English Crown in 1769 to Dartmouth, a congregational college located in the colony of New Hampshire.

---

[1] Clark Spurlock, *Education and the Supreme Court* (Urbana, Ill.: University of Illinois Press, 1955), 252 pp., is the source of much of the content of this section. The author expresses his indebtedness to him.

[2] *Trustees of Dartmouth College vs. Woodward,* 4 Wheat 518 (U.S. 1819).

Authority over the school, as set forth in the charter, was vested in a board of twelve trustees who were subject only to such state control as the colonial governor might exercise as an ex officio member of the board. The trustees were a self-perpetuating body.

In an effort to bring the college under state control, the legislature increased the trustees to twenty-one, gave the governor power to appoint them, and subordinated the board to twenty-five overseers who were state officials, also appointed by the governor. The Dartmouth trustees refused to comply with the terms of this legislation and a legal battle ensued which reached the United States Supreme Court. The Court ruled that a charter granted to a private college is a contract and that it is beyond the power of a state legislature to alter it unless those who were granted the charter concur.

Two later rulings somewhat limited the sweeping scope of this decision. One held that terms of a charter must be strictly construed and that no rights or privileges may be granted by implication. The other decision ruled that states have the power to enact general laws which reserve the right to repeal corporate charters under circumstances set forth.

It is difficult to state with certainty the effects of these decisions on education. Certainly, they enhanced the security of private institutions and assured persons interested in furthering endowments that their contributions would be used as they intended.

The only Supreme Court decision affecting apportionment of public school funds was concerned with the distribution of income from the sales of land grants for school support.[3] The Springfield, Indiana Township, contrary to state legislation, claimed it had the authority and the right to the exclusive control of its school lands and their income. The state then refused to apportion state funds to those townships which received income from federal land until other state schools had public funds equivalent in amount to invest in their schools. The Supreme Court upheld the right of the State of Indiana to withhold such funds under the conditions set forth.

The basic concept at the heart of this decision paved the way for subsequent equalization of educational opportunity on the state level through statewide collection and distribution of funds.

It has been ruled that the use of the mails to transmit instruction

---

[3] *Springfield Township* vs. *Quick,* 22 How. 56 (U.S. 1859).

and contracts is interstate commerce and under this ruling, states cannot unduly obstruct such commerce.[4]

The Court has held that while a state university may contribute to the welfare of the state by using scientific equipment imported from abroad, the state is not independent of federal power and the authority of Congress; therefore, the state must pay duty on such equipment imported for educational purposes.[5]

The same principle was reiterated in a later case which upheld the right of the federal government to collect excise taxes on admissions to athletic contests even when the revenues of such contests were to be used for education.[6] However, Congress passed Public Law No. 324 in 1954 which exempts admissions to athletic games and exhibitions from federal taxes providing they are held during the regular season for the sport involved, and providing the revenues are used exclusively for the benefit of the educational institution sponsoring the event.

A New Jersey statute was upheld which reduced salaries of employees on tenure status, holding that teachers on tenure in New Jersey were essentially under statutory provision and hence subject to subsequent legislative decisions.[7]

A related decision ruled that a dismissed teacher held a valid contract "which under Article I, Section 10, of the Federal Constitution, the Indiana Legislature could not impair by repealing the tenure law which had applied to the school where the teacher was formerly employed."[8]

The Supreme Court ruled that a reduction in payments to retired teachers set forth in previous legislation was not a violation of the contract clause of the Federal Constitution inasmuch as the earlier legislation was a statutory implementation of policy.[9] This decision draws a distinction between a pension plan supported entirely by public funds and a retirement plan supported in part by states funds and in part by contributions of the employees.

It will be noted that in four of these cases federal power was

---

4 *International Text-Book Co.* vs. *Pigg*, 217 U.S. 91, 30 Sup. Ct. 481 (1910).
5 *University of Illinois* vs. *United States*, 289 U.S. 48, 53 Sup. Ct. 509 (1933).
6 *Allen* vs. *Regents of the University System of Georgia*, 304 U.S. 439, 58 Sup. Ct. 980 (1938).
7 *Phelps* vs. *Board of Education*, 300 U.S. 319, 57 Sup. Ct. 483 (1937).
8 *Indiana ex rel. Anderson* vs. *Brand*, 303 U.S. 95, 58 Sup. Ct. 43 (1938).
9 *Dodge* vs. *Board of Education of Chicago*, 302 U.S. 74, 58 Sup. Ct. 98 (1937).

held to supersede state power; three cases upheld state power, and one upheld the rights of a citizen.

Cases arising under the Bill of Rights. In these instances, a person challenged some action on the grounds that it denied constitutional guarantees of religious freedom, nonestablishment of religion, freedom of speech, or freedom of the press.

For example, the United States Supreme Court upheld the last will and testament of Stephen Girard which provided for the endowment of a college on condition that ministers and missionaries were excluded from the premises of the college. This provision was not viewed as being derogatory to the Christian religion.[10]

A Louisiana law which provided free textbooks from public funds to children in private schools was contested before the Supreme Court. The Court asserted that the school children and not the schools were the beneficiaries of such funds. The statute was upheld on these grounds.[11]

Another case hinging on the same question tested a New Jersey law which provided free transportation to children attending parochial schools. The Court ruled that this act was not unconstitutional and enlarged upon the theory set forth in the Cochran case, that the child and not the parochial school was the beneficiary of this act.[12]

The right of a state to compel male students enrolled in the state university to take military training has been sustained.[13] A similar case in principle, but involving the religious beliefs of a student, occurred at the University of California.[14] The Supreme Court ruled that inasmuch as the student was not compelled to attend the university, in choosing to do so he must comply with the requirement that all able male students take military training even though contrary to his religious beliefs.

Two contradictory decisions regarding the compulsory salute to the flag have been rendered by the United States Supreme Court. The first case upheld a school board rule of a Pennsylvania school district that students must salute the American flag as a condition

---

10 *Vidal* vs. *Girard's Executors*, 2 How. 127 (U.S. 1844).

11 *Cochran* vs. *Louisiana State Board of Education*, 281 U.S. 370, 50 Sup. Ct. 335 (1930).

12 *Everson* vs. *Board of Education*, 330 U.S. 1, 67 Sup. Ct. 504 (1947).

13 *Pearson* vs. *Coale*, 290 U.S. 597, 54 Sup. Ct. 131 (1933).

14 *Hamilton* vs. *Regents of the University of California*, 293 U.S. 245, 55 Sup. Ct. 197 (1934).

of school attendance.[15] Later the Court held that a rule of the West Virginia State Board of Education which required all students to salute the flag and recite the Pledge of Allegiance if they were to attend school violated the First Amendment of the Constitution guaranteeing freedom of religion.[16]

Continuing the trend of cases involving religion and the schools, the Court ruled that religious instruction during the public school day held in public school buildings as then practiced in the schools of Champaign, Illinois, amounted to the establishment of a religion which was contrary to provisions of the First and Fourteenth Amendments to the Federal Constitution.[17] This decision was couched in such general terms and so limited to the specific facts of the case that its general significance was difficult to establish.

Four years later, two other cases were heard by the United States Supreme Court which dealt with the same issue. In the first case, the Court refused to rule on the validity of a New Jersey law requiring certain Bible readings in the public schools for lack of jurisdiction and thus left the state free to maintain the practice.[18] During the same year, the Court upheld a New York statute, an action of the Board of Education of the City of New York, which provided for a released time program of religious instruction during public school hours but away from public school buildings.[19] These provisions were viewed as not being in conflict with the First Amendment to the Constitution establishing freedom of worship and forbidding the establishment of a state religion.

The New York City Board of Education was denied authority to censor educational materials offensive to certain religious groups on grounds that provisions of the First and Fourteenth Amendments would be violated.[20] Specifically, it held that the State of New York could not act through a local Board of Education to censor a motion picture found to be sacrilegious as defined by some religious groups.

Two cases reached the Supreme Court in 1952 which dealt with the constitutionality of legislation concerned with beliefs of teachers

---

[15] *Minersville School District* vs. *Gobitis,* 310 U.S. 586, 60 Sup. Ct. 1011 (1940).

[16] *West Virginia State Board of Education* vs. *Barnette,* 319 U.S. 624, 63 Sup. Ct. 1178 (1943).

[17] *Illinois ex rel. McCollum* vs. *Board of Education,* 333 U.S. 203, 68 Sup. Ct. 461 (1948).

[18] *Doremus* vs. *Board of Education,* 342 U.S. 429, 72 Sup. Ct. 394 (1952).

[19] *Zorach* vs. *Clauson,* 343 U.S. 306, 72 Sup. Ct. 679 (1952).

[20] *Burstyn* vs. *Wilson,* 343 U.S. 495, 72 Sup. Ct. 777 (1952).

deemed inimicable to the public welfare. A civil service law of New York denying employment in the public schools of the state to any member of any organization which advocates overthrowing the government by unlawful means was sustained on the grounds that no federal constitutional provision was violated.[21]

In the same year, however, the Court invalidated a statute of the Oklahoma Legislature which prescribed a loyalty oath for certain public officers and employees, including teachers. The act was voided on the grounds that it was in conflict with the due process clause set forth in the Fourteenth Amendment of the Constitution.[22] It should be pointed out that the intent of the Court was not reversed. The New York law and Oklahoma statutes were found to be different. Actually, the constitutionality of loyalty oaths was not ruled on in either case.

The United States Supreme Court decided another case involving religious practice in the public schools on June 25, 1962, in *Engel* vs. *Vitale*.[23] The Board of Regents of New York State had adopted a specific prayer and recommended that public schools use it. The Court ruled that the use of a prescribed prayer was contrary to the First Amendment which denys the right of government to establish a religion and stated that this was reinforced by the Fourteenth Amendment.

These decisions are concerned with the religious rights of the individual and rest on provisions of the Federal Constitution which establish religious freedom. The Cochran and Everson cases set an important precedent in the form of a logic for granting public funds to private schools. All except two of these cases have been decided since 1930.

Rights of individuals. Instances in which persons have challenged what they construed as denial of their rights without due process of law, or questions involving equal protection under the law, are discussed in this section. The Supreme Court decided whether rights of citizens with regard to their education were violated in five of these cases.

The power of a state to make attendance at the state university contingent upon giving up allegiance to a Greek letter fraternity

---

21 *Adler* vs. *Board of Education,* 342 U.S. 485, 72 Sup. Ct. 380 (1952).
22 *Wieman* vs. *Updegraf,* 344 U.S. 183, 73 Sup. Ct. 215 (1952).
23 *Engel* vs. *Vitale,* 82 Sup. Ct. 1261, 8 L. Ed. 2d 601.

through prohibitory state legislation was upheld by the Supreme Court in one instance.[24] The Court stated that this legislation violated no right of citizens guaranteed in the Federal Constitution.

Public officials have been supported in enforcing compulsory vaccination whether or not an epidemic exists, if statutory authority to do so had been granted.[25] The decision states that a citizen has no constitutional right to enter his child in school without a vaccination certificate if such is required by the proper enactment. Earlier cases had held similarly on the grounds that it is within the police power of the state to require such regulations regardless of the state of health in a community.

The right to attend private schools was supported by the United States Supreme Court in a famous Oregon case.[26] The ruling held that an Oregon law requiring children to attend public schools while within compulsory school age limits was void because it denied parents the right to educate their children for purposes other than those of the state, and because it deprived private schools of their property without due process of law. Another case decided under the due proces of law concept held that a state could not prohibit the teaching of foreign languages in private schools on the grounds that it would interfere with the freedom of parents to control the education of their children, and that the liberty of teachers to follow their chosen profession would be denied, thus violating freedom of the individual guaranteed under the Fourteenth Amendment.[27]

Beginning in 1899 and continuing through the present, a series of Supreme Court decisions has been rendered concerning racial segregation in public schools. The dual school systems of the southern states have been held to be in violation of the Fourteenth Amendment. The doctrine of separate but equal facilities for the races upon which the dual school systems were viewed as legal was based on a Supreme Court decision which involved transportation rather than education—the famous *Plessy* vs. *Ferguson* case.

The first of these cases held that action of county authorities in Georgia supporting a high school for white children while support-

---

24 *Waugh* vs. *Mississippi University*, 237 U.S. 589, 35 Sup. Ct. 720 (1915).

25 *Zucht* vs. *King*, 260 U.S. 174, 43 Sup. Ct. 24 (1922).

26 *Pierce* vs. *Society of the Sisters of the Holy Names of Jesus and Mary*, 268 U.S. 510, 45 Sup. Ct. 571 (1925).

27 *Meyer* vs. *Nebraska*, 262 U.S. 390, 43 Sup. Ct. 625 (1923).

ing no high school for Negro children was valid.[28] Richmond County had maintained high schools for both white and Negro children for a time; later, the County Board of Education suspended operation of the Negro school on grounds of economic necessity but continued operating the school for white children. The Court expressed reluctance, as it had in other cases, to render decisions influencing education which might suggest interference with state power to manage its own schools.

Berea College, an institution chartered by the State of Kentucky, admitted both white and Negro students and treated them without discrimination. The Legislature of Kentucky passed a law in 1904 prohibiting mixing of the races in schools. Berea College was found guilty of violating this law. The Supreme Court upheld the state statute.[29]

Martha Lum, a Chinese student and a native-born citizen of the United States, was denied admittance to Mississippi white schools and assigned to the public Negro schools in her school district. The Supreme Court held that Mississippi school authorities could properly assign the Chinese student to a Negro school without denying her equal protection of the law, if equal facilities for white and colored schools were available.[30]

A landmark decision ruled that equal opportunity for a legal education must be provided within a state's own borders to Negroes and that the requirement could not be met by the state paying tuition for attending a law school in another state.[31]

A similar case occurred in Maryland involving denial of admission to the law school of a Negro citizen. The citizen was subsequently admitted when the highest Maryland court held that if the races were to be separated, facilities must be equal.

A school segregation case involving the payment of salaries to white and Negro teachers held that white and colored public school teachers with similar qualifications and similarly situated must be paid equal salaries.[32]

---

[28] Cumming vs. County Board of Education, 175 U.S. 528, 24 Sup. Ct. 197 (1899).

[29] Berea College vs. Commonwealth of Kentucky, 211 U.S. 45, 29 Sup. Ct. 33 (1908).

[30] Gong Lum vs. Rice, 275 U.S. 78, 48 Sup. Ct. 91 (1927).

[31] Missouri ex rel. Gaines vs. Canada, 305 U.S. 337, 59 Sup. Ct. 232 (1938).

[32] Alston vs. School Board of the City of Norfolk, 311 U.S. 693, 61 Sup. Ct. 75 (1940).

A far-reaching decision held that opportunity for a legal education must be provided one race as soon as another. The Supreme Court held that under the Fourteenth Amendment (equal protection clause), Oklahoma would have to provide applicants of the Negro race a legal education equal to that provided white student applicants in its state schools and that this must be done for one race as soon as the other.[33]

Another milestone in Negro education came close to the heart of the segregation issue.[34] The Supreme Court held that a separate law school for Texas Negroes did not provide them with a legal education as good as that provided for other races by the state and held that the "equal protection clause of the Fourteenth Amendment required the University of Texas Law School to admit a qualified Negro." The *Plessy* vs. *Ferguson* doctrine of separate but equal facilities was thus overthrown for the first time.

A further important decision on the segregation issue held that an enrolled graduate student could not be segregated within a state university.[35] The Supreme Court ruled that enforced segregation of a Negro student within the university who had been properly admitted to its graduate school handicapped his pursuit of graduate work and denied him the equal protection guaranteed under the Fourteenth Amendment.

Finally, the Supreme Court ruled directly on the issue of segregation in the public schools.[36] The essence of this ruling was that segregation by races in the public schools is a violation of constitutional rights of citizens guaranteed under the Fourteenth Amendment.

In a period of a little more than half a century, the Supreme Court reversed itself on the issue of segregation in the public schools. Even as late as 1950, the Court had not abolished the *Plessy* vs. *Ferguson* doctrine of separate but equal facilities enunciated in 1896. A review of the cases leading to the 1954 decision clearly shows that the Court has been increasingly concerned with the definition of equality.

---

[33] *Sipuel* vs. *Oklahoma Board of Regents*, 332 U.S. 631, 68 Sup. Ct. 299 (1948).
[34] *Sweatt* vs. *Painter*, 339 U.S. 629, 70 Sup. Ct. 848 (1950).
[35] *McLaurin* vs. *Oklahoma State Regents*, 339 U.S. 637, 70 Sup. Ct. 851 (1950).
[36] *Brown* vs. *Board of Education of Topeka (Kansas)*, 347 U.S. 483, 74 Sup. Ct. 686 (1954), and *Bolling* vs. *Sharpe (District of Columbia)*, 347 U.S. 497, 74 Sup. Ct. 693 (1954).

A district federal court ruled in 1962 that Prince Edwards County, Virginia, could not close its schools in order to avoid a court desegregation order since the state constitution requires the state to maintain a system of public schools for the entire state. This decision may prove to be of historic significance, if upheld by higher courts, for it rules in effect that a state must provide a public school system.

State Court Decisions

Each of the fifty states has its own judicial system, with a court structure similar in many instances to that of the federal government. As has been pointed out previously, states have considerable leeway in enacting school legislation. The resultant body of school law in the various states is extensive in coverage and volume. Thus, there are numerous opportunities for differences of opinion leading to litigation. Each court decision is binding, of course, only in the state where it is rendered. However, many key decisions have affected education in other states. Only decisions considered to be of prime significance are presented here; consequently, only those reaching the state supreme court will be drawn upon. Emphasis is placed on the impact of the decisions on schools with little reference to purely legal considerations.

Authority of the state. The state courts have repeatedly upheld the doctrine that in America education is a function of the state and is, therefore, fundamentally a matter of state policy. Attempts to define the scope and quality of this policy have been undertaken by various courts from time to time. This means that the public school is essentially a state institution and not a local institution.

This doctrine is stated succinctly by the Supreme Court of Minnesota in these words: "This court so frequently has affirmed the doctrine that the maintenance of the public school is a matter of state and not local concern that it is unnecessary further to review the authorities at this date.[37] The Tennessee High Court stated:

> The public school system is a matter of state, and not local concern, and the establishment, maintenance, and control of the public schools is a legislative function. To promote the public schools, the state through the legislature, may levy taxes directly, or the state,

---

[37] *State ex rel. Board of Education of Minneapolis* vs. *Erickson,* 190 Minn. 216, 251 N.W. 519.

having, as it does, full control over its agencies, the counties, may authorize them to levy a tax, or may by statute require them to levy a tax for the establishment and maintenance of public schools ...

The exercise of the taxing power to promote a system of public schools for all of the counties does not infringe upon the right of local self government, because a public school system, like a highway system, a penal system, or a matter of public health is not purely local, but of state concern. The state is a unit, and the legislature is the state source of legislative power, from which flows the mandate of the state.[38]

The Supreme Court of New Hampshire states that,

The primary purpose of the maintenance of the common school system is the promotion of the general intelligence of the people constituting the body politic and thereby to increase the usefulness and efficiency of the citizens, upon which the government of society depends. Free schooling furnished by the state is not so much a right granted to pupils as a duty imposed upon them for the public good.[39]

A decision concerned with the functions of the state legislature in determining educational policy states that:

Essentially and intrinsically, the schools in which are educated and trained the children who are to become the rulers of the commonwealth are matters of state, and not of local jurisdiction. In such matters, the state is the unit, and the legislature the source of power. The authority over schools and school affairs is not necessarily a distributory one to be exercised by local instrumentalities; but, on the contrary, it is a central power residing in the legislature of the state. It is for the lawmaking power to determine if the authority shall be exercised by a state board of education, or distributed to county, township, or city organizations throughout the state ...

As the power over schools is a legislative one, it is not exhausted by the exercise. The legislature having tried one plan is not precluded from trying another. It has a complete choice of methods, and may change its plans as often as it deems necessary or expedient ...[40]

The definition of state responsibility for education set forth in these decisions clearly places school officers in the category of state officers and not local officers. Their manner of selection is a legis-

---

[38] *State* vs. *Meador*, 284 S.W. (Tennessee), 890.

[39] *Fogg* vs. *Board of Education*, 76 N.W. 296, 82 Atl. 173, 37 L.R.A. (N.S.) 1110, Ann. Cas. 19120. 758.

[40] *State* vs. *Haworth*, 122 Ind. 462, 23 N.E. 946, 7 L.R.A. 240.

lative function. This means that school officers need not reside in the district where they hold office unless specifically required to do so by the legislature.

It has been held that the authority to legislate cannot be delegated to any other body by the legislature; but, the legislature may create agencies and empower them to carry out its policies as set forth in legislation. In short, legislatures may delegate administrative powers but not legislative powers.

School districts. States have not attempted to administer the schools directly. Within constitutional limits, the state is free to create and delegate power to such agencies and units as it may deem advisable for the actual organization, administration, and supervision of education. Legislatures may require existing civil districts such as townships, towns, cities and counties to assume designated responsibilities for establishing and operating schools. Should it choose to do so, the legislature can create entirely new local school districts, ignoring existing civil units.

School districts may be abolished at the will of the legislature and new ones created according to its wishes. The residents who live in a school district do not have to consent to the establishment of the district, and the state may establish districts of as many kinds as it chooses. Regardless of the types of districts the legislature may elect to create for the purpose of carrying out its educational policies, such districts are subject to the control of the legislature and no other agency, within constitutional limitations. A local school district has no rights, inherent or otherwise, except those which are conferred upon it by the state legislature. These rights and powers and how they are to be exercised are defined by the legislature and these may be changed or eliminated at the will of the legislature.

Municipalities are usually established and governed under charters granted by state legislatures. Generally, such charters bestow upon municipal governments freedom to control their local affairs under their own government, subject to the limitations of the charter and legislation which may be of statewide application. These charters usually make provisions for the creation and administration of a school system within the municipality.

Municipal governments are created essentially for purposes of local self-government and are not instruments of state policy. The school district, as has been pointed out, is an instrument for carrying out state policy and serves as a subdivision of the state for this purpose. Whenever a conflict arises between the provisions of a home-rule charter and the constitution or legislative policy of the state, such provisions are invalid. It has been ruled, however, that in case of a special charter for a particular city, charter provisions are applicable even though they may be in conflict with the general statutes on the subject.[41]

School board members in some cities are appointed by the mayor, but this authority gives the mayor no legal control whatsoever over policies of the school board. It has been held that school board members are state officers and not officers of the municipality, that school districts are a part of the state school system and not an institution of the municipality.[42]

The courts are in agreement that a school district may exercise the following powers and no others: "(1) Those expressly granted by statute, (2) those fairly and necessarily implied in the powers expressly granted, and (3) those essential to the accomplishment of the objects of the corporation." [43]

Financial responsibility. The levying of state taxes is the prerogative of the legislative branch of government. Its freedom to tax is limited only by its own state constitution and the Federal Constitution. It is free to view the state as a tax unit, or it may create subdivisions of the state such as school districts, municipal corporations, and other units of local government, and confer upon them the power to tax. It can also withdraw this power to tax.

The Supreme Court of Kansas has stated:

> The authority to levy taxes is an extraordinary one. It is never left to implication unless it is a necessary implication. Its warrant must be clearly found in the act of the legislature. Any other rule might lead to great wrong and oppression, and when there is a reasonable doubt as to the existence, the right must be denied. Therefore, to say that the right is in doubt is to deny its existence.[44]

Other court decisions uphold the same principle. School districts

---

[41] *Board of Education of City of Minneapolis* vs. *Houghton,* 181 Minn. 576, 233 N.W. 834.

[42] *Barnes* vs. *District of Columbia,* 91 U.S. 540, 23 L. Ed. 440.

[43] Newton Edwards, *The Courts and the Public Schools,* rev. ed. (Chicago: The University of Chicago Press, 1955), p. 146.

[44] *Marion and McPherson Railway Company* vs. *Alexander,* 63 Kans. 72, 64 Pac. 978.

thus cannot levy taxes for school purposes unless the power to do so has been given them or has been implied through the assignment of some responsibility which demands the power to tax.

It has been ruled that:

> When a municipal body, or a county, or a school district levies taxes for school purposes, the tax so levied is a state and not a municipal, county, or district tax, although it may be levied and collected by the municipal, or county, or district officer. The fact that the tax is levied and collected for the state by the agencies of the state appointed for that purpose does not deprive it of its character as a state tax.[45]

This has been interpreted to mean that school districts and municipalities may be required by the state to levy taxes for school purposes against their will.

The Kansas Court held that:

> The matter of education is one of public interest which concerns all the people of the state and is therefore subject to the control of the legislature . . . It is conceded that the legislature has full power to compel local organizations of the state to maintain common schools, and as schools of a higher grade are authorized by the constitution, no reason is seen why such organizations may not be compelled to maintain high schools.[46]

On various occasions the courts have ruled that a school board has authority to levy such taxes as it judges are required to achieve the purposes of the local schools as long as no prescribed tax limit is exceeded. The Illinois Court so ruled in the following words:

> The power of taxation, altogether legislative and in no degree judicial, is committed by the legislature in the matter of schools to the directors of school districts. If the directors refuse to perform their duties, the court can compel them. If they transcend their powers, the courts can restrain them. If they misjudge their power, the court can correct them. But if they exercise their unquestionable powers unwisely, there is no judicial remedy.[47]

The principle that a state legislature is empowered to levy a statewide school tax and distribute the proceeds as it deems wise providing only that the criteria of distribution be applied alike to all

---

[45] City of Louisville vs. Board of Education, 154 Ky. 316, 157 S.W. 379.
[46] State vs. Freeman, 61 Kans. 90, 58 Pac. 959, 47 L.R.A. 67.
[47] People vs. Scott, 300, Ill. 290, 133 N.E. 299.

districts has been upheld in more than one case. This principle has also been sustained by a Supreme Court decision regarding the distribution of income from federal land grants for school purposes.

Authority of the state to tax for school purposes is clearly set forth in a Supreme Court case from Maine in the following words:

> The legislature has the right under the constitution to impose an equal rate of taxation upon all properties in the state, including the property in unorganized townships, for the purpose of distributing the proceeds thereof among the cities, towns, and plantations for common school purposes . . .
>
> The method of distributing the proceeds of such a tax rests in the wise discretion and sound judgment of the legislature. If this discretion is unwisely exercised, the remedy is with the people and not with the court . . .[48]

It will be noted that in addition to the principle of giving a state the power to tax, the responsibility of the state to determine the method of apportioning school funds is also upheld in the same decision. Apportionment procedures are usually prescribed by state legislatures. The actual process of apportioning, however, is often delegated to the chief state school officer or the state board of education. Some states grant authority to the officer or the board to approve or withhold some types of funds for purposes of enforcing state educational requirements. Efforts are made to define objective measures to be used in apportioning funds in order to prevent the use of too much freedom by awarding agencies.

The authority of school districts to issue bonds originates from statutory provisions or from such authority as may be implied by the purposes which underlie creation of the district. Authority of a school district to issue negotiable instruments is somewhat more limited. For example, the power to borrow money does not imply power to issue negotiable bonds. In any event, the legislature is the source of school district authority to issue bonds. However, the procedures outlined by the statute in the exercise of this authority must be followed. Proceeds from the bonds must be used for the purposes set forth in the issue.

Liability of school districts and school officers. School districts, like municipalities, cannot be held liable for injuries to pupils resulting from the negligence of employees of the district, unless a

---

[48] *Sawyer* vs. *Gilmore,* 109 Me. 169, 83 Atl. 673.

statute makes the district liable. A statute permitting or authorizing a school district to sue and be sued does not necessarily abrogate immunity for accidents growing out of negligence of employees, but the statute must be written in clear and specific language. New York courts, however, have held that school boards may be held liable for negligence in performing duties imposed by law.

State courts have repeatedly ruled that school officers cannot be held to personal liability for their official acts. School officers are not liable for injuries caused by errors in their judgment as long as they act in good faith and within their responsibilities. Where duties are prescribed by law which require no exercise of judgment in their performance, in contrast to the quasi judicial duties referred to above, the school officer may be liable for injuries sustained due to his failure to perform these duties properly. School officers are not held personally liable for failure to perform a duty or for negligent performance where the duties are imposed upon them while acting in their corporate capacity. If a law places a duty upon a school board, it is on the board as a legal body or entity rather than on the board members separately as individuals.

It has been established that teachers are not public officers but are employees. As such, they are personally liable for the consequences of negligence while performing their duties as teachers. The law demands that a teacher exercise the proper care of any reasonable person when performing his duties. Therefore, should he pursue action which a reasonably prudent person would view as a threat to the safety of pupils, he will be held guilty if there is injury to pupils.

Teacher qualifications. State courts have upheld the authority of the state to prescribe qualifications for teachers. Contracts to teach are not valid unless the individual possesses a certificate of qualification as required by law. It has been held that even though the teacher actually renders services under such a contract, he cannot hold the board of education to payment for these services. Qualifications for state certification are set forth in state legislation or state board regulations and the responsibility for issuing certificates is delegated to some officer or agency, frequently the state department of education.

A certificate to teach has been construed as a license granted by the state and not a contract between the state and the teacher.

Therefore, a certificate may be revoked by the state, or the state may define new and additional requirements for the holders of certificates. But, if a statute outlines causes for which certificates may be revoked, a certificate cannot be revoked for any other causes.

Employment of teachers. The board of education cannot delegate the authority to contract with teachers, not even to its own school superintendent. The principle is well established that a school board, or other corporate bodies charged with performing duties requiring the exercise of discretion, cannot delegate these duties to others. But such a corporate body can delegate to an official or a committee the power to determine eligible employees for contracts, to draw up tentative contracts, and to present such to the corporate body for approval. Thus, school superintendents recommend personnel to boards of education for appointments, but no contract is valid unless approved by the board.

Teacher welfare. Many states have adopted legislation to provide permanent tenure for teachers. Such statutes set forth the requirements which must be met if tenure is secured and outline the causes for which a teacher may be dismissed, usually describing the procedure to be followed. Most court decisions have held that tenure provisions do not constitute a contract between the state and the teachers. Since an act of the legislature is construed as defining current legislative policy, subsequent legislatures are free to change this policy, unless a contract is involved.

Therefore, the wording of a tenure law is of extreme importance since a state can legally create a contract which involves the tenure of teachers. In that event, a subsequent legislative act could not repeal or amend the statute. But tenure legislation does not limit school officials in determining positions to be established and maintained, or what is to be taught. Should it become desirable to abolish positions for good reason, a school board is empowered to do so even though it means the loss of employment to teachers on tenure. In such cases, teachers having tenure are generally entitled to preference in reappointment if and when vacancies occur. Tenure laws do not prevent boards of education from making reasonable changes in the salaries earned by teachers, as long as no discrimination is involved.

The authority of states to establish teacher retirement systems has been upheld by state courts. Such systems may be financed entirely by state contributions or by joint contributions from the state and the employees. School districts may establish retirement systems if authorized to do so by state statute. Establishment by a state of a retirement system does not within itself denote a contract between the state and the teachers. If the state retirement system can be classified as a pension plan, the system can be changed by the legislature as it deems appropriate without teachers entering a valid claim of violation of contractual rights.

Determining whether or not a teacher retirement plan creates a contract between the state and the teacher is sometimes a difficult matter. In such cases, the actual wording of the law involved is important, as is the attitude of the particular court on such matters. Since the Federal Constitution prohibits states from passing laws which impair the obligations of contracts, if a contractual relationship is stated in the legislation, the tenure law in effect does establish a contract with the member teacher. Some courts have held that if the statute requires teachers to have a part of their salary paid into the retirement fund, a contractual relationship exists. On the other hand, some state courts have ruled the reverse.

Compulsory school attendance. Authority of state legislatures to pass compulsory school attendance laws has been challenged in several cases but in all instances has been upheld. According to the courts, compulsory attendance does not confer a benefit upon the parents or even primarily upon the child, but rather upon the state in that the well-being and safety of the state demands the education of its citizens.

Punishment of students. A number of cases hold that a board of education has the power to expel or suspend any student from school for disobedience of board regulations. However, regulations must be reasonable and must fall within the jurisdiction of the board. Hence, the proper dismissal of a student hinges on what is defined as violation of a reasonable rule. A board of education may either suspend or expel a pupil from school even when no specific rule has been violated. This recognizes the fact that it would be impossible to develop a set of rules which would cover every possibility of violations which might interfere with the well-being of the school.

Courts agree that when a parent sends his child to school, he delegates authority to the teacher to discipline the student in the interest of appropriate order and conduct in the school. This does not, however, give the teacher the right the parent holds to punish for all offenses. Such punishment must fall within the responsibility of the teacher in conducting his work effectively. Teachers may inflict corporal punishment for offenses within the jurisdiction of the school as long as the punishment is reasonable. Such punishment may extend to acts committed off the school grounds, the nature of the act rather than the place where it is committed determining the right to punish. Obviously, the definition of reasonable corporate punishment is difficult. Several decisions have ruled that a teacher will not be held liable unless permanent or lasting injury is caused by the punishment, or that punishment was delivered with malicious intent.[49]

Summary

Decisions of both federal courts and state courts have profoundly affected the course of education in this country. The two classifications of decisions are not as discrete as may be implied from this statement, inasmuch as many cases decided by the Supreme Court were initiated in state courts. Such cases involved questions concerning violation of one or more provisions of the United States Constitution, else they would not have been eligible for consideration by the Supreme Court.

Decisions made by the United States Supreme Court have generally involved application of either the general welfare clause, the Bill of Rights, or the Fourteenth Amendment. The question most often argued has been whether or not a given state law or practice violated the rights of the individual or whether rights were denied without due process of law. The result of these decisions has been to define more precisely powers of the states to implement the concept that education is a function of the state.

Major restrictions placed on the states by these decisions are as follows:

1. No legislative enactment is constitutional which impairs established contractual relationships;

---

[49] The author has drawn heavily on *The Courts and the Public Schools* by Newton Edwards for much of the major content of the section on state courts and hereby expresses appreciation to him.

2. No legislative enactment or practice sanctioned by the state can abridge the right of the individual to freedom of religious choice and worship;

3. No legislative enactment or practice supported by the state can deny equal protection for all citizens irrespective of race, color, or background;

4. The state cannot exercise its police power in ways to deny any citizen his rights except under the due process of law clause.

Federal court decisions affecting education have been indirect in their application because no reference is made to education in the Federal Constitution. This limitation has not served to unduly restrict the influence of the Supreme Court on education.

State courts have been much more involved in litigation concerning education. Most states in carrying out their responsibilities for establishing and maintaining public school systems have passed voluminous bodies of law pertaining to education. An enormous body of state court decisions has been accumulated. Almost all phases of education have at one time or another been the subject of state court action. The decision of a state court is binding only in its own state. There are many similarities in the nature of cases tried and in the character of decisions rendered by courts of the various states.

In general, it seems safe to say that the following generalizations are valid:

1. There is general agreement among the various court decisions that the states does have responsibility for providing and maintaining public education for its citizens and the necessary authority to do so.

2. State legislatures are fully empowered to pass legislation of any sort concerning the establishment, control, maintenance, and support of public schools in the state, except such as may be restricted by the United States Constitution or the state constitution.

3. State legislatures are free to delegate some of their power and responsibility for public education to state agencies it may create or designate for this purpose and to local agencies which it may create or delegate for this purpose. The state, however, cannot free itself of reasonable responsibility for the proper exercise of delegated powers and responsibilities to these agencies and it must set forth the limits under which these agencies perform the responsibilities delegated to them.

4. The public school is a state and not a local institution and as such the local government can exercise no authority over the schools within its boundaries except such as are delegated to it by the state. In practice, the public school program is a partnership program between the state

and the local school district. The local school district is a creature of the state and exists to exercise for the state specific powers allocated to it concerned with organizing and administering the schools. Although these districts may be created independently of existing civil districts, or their limits may be coterminous with municipal or county districts, they are creatures of the state and maintain identities separate from the local civil districts.

5. School districts being corporate entities cannot be held liable for acts of negligence by their employees while acting in their official capacity, except where state law specifically imposes such liability. Only three states have such laws, but some authorities assert that courts are recognizing to an increasing degree both the responsibility and liability of the state and the agencies it creates to serve its purposes.[50]

---

[50] Taken with minor adaptations from Morphet, Johns, and Reller, *Educational Administration, Concepts, Practices, and Issues* (Englewood Cliffs, N.J.: Prentice-Hall, Inc., 1959), p. 43.

CHAPTER VI

The Executive Branch of Government

There has been little study of the role of the executive branch of government in education. No inference should be drawn, however, that its influence is unimportant. The major functions of the executive division of government are to exert leadership in the development of public policy and to assist in the execution of this policy.

Education has always been considered of such importance that it has been the subject of much public policy. The executive leader is in position to exert great influence on the determination of policy with respect to education through his work with the legislative branch of government and through other means open to him, such as his power of appointment.

The philosophy of government and government service reflected by the work of the executive is of great importance. Espousal of Jefferson's view that the best government does the least governing means a different type of policy as compared to ones favored by persons who believe the power of government should be used as a positive force to serve the best interests of the people. The party system makes it possible for the people to choose government officials on the basis of their position on public problems and issues.

The personal qualities of the executive help determine his influence on public policy. Historically, strong, vigorous, and dynamic executives have wielded much power in determining government policy, while the weaker, timid, and less aggressive executives have been largely ineffective. It would be hard to overestimate the importance of the leadership function in determining public policy.

The executive may implement policy successfully or poorly, depending upon his intentions and abilities. His influence on educational policy will vary accordingly. The power of the executive over policy may be viewed as a fluid one depending on such factors as his willingness to act, his performance under pressure, what is expected of him, and his own beliefs and values.

The Federal Executive Branch
of Government

There is nothing in the Federal Constitution which gives the executive branch of government responsibility for or authority over education. Therefore, influence of the executive stems from implied powers, as is true of the legislative and judicial branches of government.

The President.   The Office of the President of the United States carries with it tremendous prestige. The holder of this office wields great power, some of which is expressly granted by the Constitution.

Among these powers is that of appointment. The President appoints the members of his cabinet, members of the judiciary, and thousands of other government officials. While many of these appointments must be confirmed by the Senate, the President is nevertheless in position to influence greatly the policy of government through the character of these appointments.

The veto power gives the President another strong source of influence. The veto usually enables the President to exercise final control over legislation since his veto is seldom overridden.

The President is in position to affect legislation by virtue of the views he holds as well as those held by the party of which he is a member. He works with legislative leaders in order to develop the legislative program. He usually works actively in the interest of commitments concerning needed policies and legislation. His position on education will help determine the policy of the national government on this subject.

Another important influence on education is the implementation of policies of the government. The extent to which the President seeks full implementation and the measures he uses are of crucial importance. For example, use of the presidential power to send troops to enforce a court order which has engendered bitterness will yield quite a different outcome than would reliance on words of exhortation.

The Department of Health, Education, and Welfare.   Official responsibility of the executive branch for education is vested in a department of the President's Cabinet—the Department of Health, Education, and Welfare.

The Commissioner of Education. Immediate administrative responsibility for education in the federal government is in the office of the United States Commissioner of Education. This office is in the Department of Health, Education, and Welfare. The Commissioner is appointed by the President. He serves as executive head of the United States Office of Education.

The Office of Education. This office was established in 1867 as the Department of Education. It was placed in the Department of Health, Education, and Welfare when the department was created in 1953. Hence, education is represented officially in the President's Cabinet by the Secretary of this department.

Unlike state departments of education, the Office of Education is not responsible for a school system. It is responsible for administering those federal education programs which are assigned to it. The duties assigned to this office are: collecting facts about the schools, organizing and analyzing these facts in order to present the state of education in the nation, distributing such information, and serving in whatever way seems feasible in promoting educational development in the nation.

The office has always recognized that the control of education is a function of the state. Hence, it has sought to aid school systems in the development of adequate education programs. The office is responsible for the allocation of federal funds to land-grant colleges and universities, administering federal funds, approving state plans for vocational education, and administering vocational rehabilitation programs for disabled persons.

The office carries on an extensive program of study and publications. It publishes the *Biennial Survey of Education,* the most complete statistical study of education available, and an official monthly magazine entitled *School Life.* Other publications include numerous reports covering a wide variety of educational topics which are used extensively by educators and laymen.

In recent years, the Office of Education has greatly enlarged its consultative and advisory services. Specialists on the staff represent most areas of education and are available to work with school systems and attendance centers on programs with which their specializations deal. Conferences on educational programs and needs are sponsored by the Office of Education. Its staff also assists in making various kinds of studies of education.

Functions of the office which reflect growth in the scope of its activities are: administering the National Defense Education Act, the Cooperative Research Program, the school assistance program to federally affected areas, and administering grants for the training of teachers of mentally retarded children.

In spite of this far-flung program, however, the Office of Education has no responsibility for many activities of the federal government directly connected with education. The several schools established and maintained by the federal government are connected in no way with the Office of Education. The military colleges and universities are also operated independently of the Office of Education. Numerous government agencies and departments which have educational programs carry them on largely without reference to the Office of Education.

The Attorney General. A second position in the President's Cabinet which influences education is the office of the Attorney General.

Relationships to the judiciary and the legal powers ascribed to the department are of special significance when schools become involved in matters requiring interpretations of the law. The effects of such interpretation on educational practice may be considerable. This department has a unique role when court decisions modify practice and adjudicate disputes. It may be authorized to monitor performance in light of court decisions and court orders. Where rights are violated, the office may become a party to litigation.

A perennial question. The question of extending federal support to education has been before Congress almost constantly during the past two decades. The role of the executive branch of the federal government in education has assumed added significance in light of this question. A notable example of executive influence occurred in the early days of the Kennedy Administration when the powerful House Rules Committee was enlarged for the purpose of making it a more liberal body, thus enhancing the chances of increasing federal support to education.

The State Executive Branch
of Government

Much that has been said about the federal executive branch of government and education applies to a great extent to most of the

fifty states. There are some major differences, however, due largely
to the fact that state constitutions make acceptance by the state of
responsibility for education mandatory.

The State Governor. The governor as chief executive holds a
position within the state comparable in many ways to the President's
position in the nation. He does have less freedom of choice with
respect to educational policy because education is a function of the
state. The governorship is closer to the people than the presidency
and the people in a state are usually less diverse in opinions, interests, and attitudes than the population of the nation as a whole.

The chief executive of a state has great power, although his
powers vary significantly from one state to another. He has extensive authority for the appointment and removal of personnel, for
law enforcement, for the administration of state affairs, and for the
supervision of state government. He also has considerable authority
over state finances, although this authority is generally carefully
spelled out in law.

Like the President, the governor is elected on a platform which
presumably forms the basis for the development of the policy un-
derlying his administration. He works extensively with leaders in
the legislature in the development of a legislative program. He uses
his influence to secure enactment of legislation which he favors,
and he uses the veto power to keep legislation which he does not
favor from becoming law.

Obviously, the stand taken by the governor and his party on
problems and issues is of considerable importance in determining
state policy during an administration. The effectiveness of the governor in determining policy is related to his aggressiveness, his
capacity to lead, his forcefulness, and his convictions. These convictions include the philosophy of government and government
service which guide his actions.

There are many illustrations of a wide variety of influences on
education wielded by chief executives of states. In more than one
state, the chief executive has allocated balances accumulated in the
state treasury to the support of schools, usually to increase the
salaries of teachers or for capital outlay purposes. One governor
appropriated funds to establish and operate several trade schools.

Governors frequently run for office on platforms which make
specific commitments to education. They may pledge themselves to

increase general school support, increase salaries, establish new institutions of higher learning, or they may run on a platform recommending no additional school support. Thus, the voters have an opportunity to influence educational policy on the state level.

The governor's position on such issues as education for mentally retarded children, ownership of school buses, free textbooks, and subjects to be taught in the schools is likely to determine the nature of decisions with respect to these matters.

Other state executives. The attorney general may perform state level functions similar to those served by the United States Attorney General. Sometimes other state administrative officers are involved in educational matters through the enforcement of standards such as those concerning school building construction, the safety of school children, and health measures. The collection and distribution of school funds is usually handled by the established fiscal agencies of the state.

As pointed out in Chapter IV, states have created executive and administrative structures for discharging their responsibilities for education. The state board of education, the chief state school officer, and the state department of education thus came into being. They might have been treated here if structural significance within the pattern of state government had been deemed more important than their impact on the schools.

Local Government Executives

Most local governments originated from general constitutional or legislative provisions which create the structure of the local units and define their powers and responsibilities. There is no local government except as created by the state to serve the purposes of the state.

Local government is closest to the people and is often far removed from the state capitol. Therefore, in an operational sense, local government derives much of its dynamics from the local community although the structure through which these dynamics express themselves is created by the state. Decisions at the local level concerning education are much more intimate and personal than those made at either state or federal levels. The selection of a school superintendent, a school principal, a teacher, or a decision on where to locate a school building often are the personal concern of many people in the community. What is to be taught takes on new and more intimate meaning in the local community. Here controversies may arise over educational practice, or over the materials of instruction used in the school. Such decisions, however, must be made among the choices granted by the state. These choices vary substantially among the different states.

Theoretically, these and other questions affecting educational policy at the local level are answered through the local board of education and the administrative staff of the local school system. In a more practical sense, decisions made may utilize the formal structure of the schools to reflect the weight of opinion in the community. This opinion may be more powerful in the local setting than state law and state regulations.

Educational practice maintained on the basis of tradition may continue in local school districts long after legislation has been enacted making such practice illegal. Illegal practice can be corrected only by the initiation of appropriate action. In many cases, such action may not be initiated for years. Meanwhile the weight of tradition becomes greater. Unpublished studies of school boards in one state revealed that in some counties school board members still acted as representatives of subdivisions of the county which were no longer legally in existence, and that as such each member served virtually as a district school superintendent despite the fact that three generations earlier the law of the state had been modified to render such practice illegal.

It is in the local setting that the widely acclaimed flexibility of education to meet differing needs among communities derives meaning. Much diversity in American education is due to the amount of freedom left to the local communities by states in making decisions concerning educational matters. Here, provincialism can be found at its worst and the imagination and ingenuity that produces new and better educational practices can be found at its best.

It is also in local communities that nepotism is most likely to flourish. The power structure of the communities within the school system may control the schools to a very considerable extent. Thus, the appointment of relatives to positions in the schools by board members or through the influence of board members is not uncommon. Local politics at its worst and its best may be found reflected in educational practices within school districts. Such politics may influence not only the appointment of teachers but also the selection of bus drivers, the direction of bus routes, and the places of business where local school funds are expended.

The virtues of local control of education are generally considered to far outweigh the improper uses of local autonomy which occur. Escape from a national system of education with its possible rigidity and uniformity is perhaps one reward. The utilization of the normal interest of the parent in his child's education and the dynamics of community interaction in educational development is another reward.

Any assessment of government influences on education would be incomplete without taking into account the influence within local school districts which determine educational policy in the school communities. These forces are responsible for the character of decisions which go far toward shaping educational opportunity within the autonomy the state grants the local school districts.

Summary

The executive branch of government at all levels can exercise much power in the formulation and implementation of educational policy and therefore the character of educational opportunity.

The Chief Executive of the United States wields tremendous influence by virtue of his position. His influence may be expressed in support of, or opposition to, legislation concerning the schools, through his appointments of personnel, his veto power, and the quality of his leadership. This influence is also expressed in the implementation of educational policies and through official statements on educational needs.

Other officials of the executive branch may exert influence in similar ways, though to a lesser degree. The office of the Attorney General is unique in its power over education. As the watch dog of the rights of the people and as the legal branch of government, its functions are of much importance in the formulation and execution of educational policy, especially where laws are violated or the rights of people are in question.

The Office of Education, located in the Department of Health, Education, and Welfare, and administered by the United States

Commissioner of Education is the major administrative agency of the federal government concerned with public education. This office performs multiple services including those of conducting important studies, publishing valuable reports and documents, providing consultative services to state and local school systems, and administering educational programs financed by the federal government such as the National Defense Education Act and the Vocational Education Program. The Office of Education seems to be growing in the scope of its activities and influencing education to a greater degree than ever before.

The executive branch of a state government exerts similar influences on education within state boundaries. However, the fifty states differ in substantial ways and the power of the executive branch of government therefore varies among the states. The governor as the chief executive of a state is a powerful figure by virtue of the status of his office and by virtue of the extensive powers given to him in most states. The governor participates actively in determining educational policy on the state level, and he has major responsibilities for carrying out adopted policies. The attitude of the governor on educational matters as well as the attitude of the party he represents are of primary importance in educational development. The appointive powers of the governor and his veto powers may be significant in the formulation of educational policy.

Other administrative and executive officials have some responsibility for education also. Their points of view and their philosophy of education may be important considerations in developing state educational programs. The attorney general and his staff represent the state in matters involving legal services, including those affecting education.

The government of local communities is also important in education. Although local government is legally a creature of the states for convenience, it has freedom to exercise much initiative in developing and carrying out policies regarding education in its communities. The local government being closer to the people is much more sensitive to public opinion and the wishes of the people. Hence, mores, provincialism, and the more creative local dynamics can be reflected in these school systems.

CHAPTER VII

Issues

Education has been a primary concern of the American people since the original colonies were founded. It is therefore natural that the power of government has been used to establish and maintain public schools. No clear-cut plan for the participation of government in education has been instituted in this country. Instead, the relationships of government to education have been developed through evolutionary processes. In spite of the lack of overall policy, certain guides have evolved on the basis of experiences which are generally accepted, many of which have legal sanction.

One of the most important guides makes education a function of the respective states. Wide discretion in the degree and manner of exercising this function is left to the states. The states have accepted responsibility for education and have made provisions for it within this frame of reference. A far-reaching principle is that states in providing education for their citizens must do so within the bounds of federal guarantees of rights of the individual.

Another important principle is that all three levels of government participate in education, but within the limits of the concept that education is a function of the state. Not only do federal, state, and local governments take part in educational affairs, but the executive, legislative, and judicial branches of government each have their impact on the schools.

The ends sought through education have served as a major guide to the role of government in public education. Individual enhancement and social betterment are the broad goals. The right to an education is viewed as the heritage of every individual regardless of need or station in life. The concept of equality of educational opportunity has been of far-reaching significance in this country. Hence, schools are adaptable to the needs of individuals and communities as well as to changing cultural conditions. Therefore, variability and heterogeneity in education are cultivated in America. A viewpoint unique to this country is that education is under lay control, a part of which resides in local communities where schools exist.

These and other concepts have not been developed without trial and error, differences of opinion, and controversy. They have emerged through the resolution of problems and issues which are characteristic of a growing democracy. Problems and issues remain. Some are of long standing, others are relatively new. There are various ways of defining these issues. An effort has been made here to define them on a level which permits the examination of their interrelationships.

The Issue of Responsibility

Although legal responsibility for education clearly resides with the state, the actual exercise of this responsibility is not as clear-cut as the placing of legal responsibility indicates. Sometimes overlapping jurisdictions appear to exist and the joint exercise of responsibility is not uncommon.

No state except Hawaii has chosen to discharge its functions in education wholly through state agencies. Other states create local school districts and delegate to them much of the actual responsibility for establishing, organizing, and maintaining public schools. As stated previously, school districts function under grants of power from the states. In a practical sense, school districts have been free to exercise not only powers expressly given them by the state but also those which were not forbidden by the state.

Confusion has sometimes resulted from unclear definitions of powers exercised directly by the state and powers allocated to the school district. Both states and local districts have shared this confusion. As a matter of legal principle, however, states have complete authority over schools if they choose to exercise it, with the exception of practices which violate constitutional provisions.

Probably the greatest confusion and misunderstanding regarding responsibility for education lies in the area of federal participation. In a strict legal sense, the national government may be viewed as having no responsibility for education, except where court decisions are involved. However, acceptance of responsibility is implicit in the extensive support which is provided.

No policy exists which clarifies the nature and level of responsibility of the three levels of government to education.

The Issue of Control

Responsibility and control are ordinarily presumed to go hand-in-hand. They are often seen as two sides of the same coin. Their interrelationships appear to be obvious since it is difficult to see how responsibility can be discharged without a considerable measure of control, or how control can be exercised without commensurate responsibility.

The principle is well established that control over education resides in the state, otherwise it would be difficult, if not impossible, to implement the concept that education is a function of the state. The fact that states delegate much of their responsibility for education to local school districts means that a certain amount of control will be delegated also. These relationships are sometimes unclear and as a result misunderstandings arise and controversy may occur.

Some unique aspects of American public education are found in practices involving responsibility and control. Accepted concepts of responsibility for control in political science and in business are not always the same in education. The basic structure of the public schools, by definition and allocation of authority, separates them from other phases of local government and, therefore, they are not responsible to local government. This has created much debate and some authorities in public administration believe that the control of education should not differ from the control of the fire department or the police department in municipal government.

The mere fact that Congress has chosen to allocate funds for the support of education raises questions of control. The initial grant of public lands for the support of education was for general support and therefore did not produce fear of federal control. Subsequent appropriations in support of special educational purposes have been seriously questioned on the grounds that control is implicit in such support. To be sure, the land grants stimulated interest in public schools and doubtless served to generate initiative for action on state and local levels. This is not the same as the result achieved by appropriations which single out and strengthen selected areas of school programs such as vocational education or special education.

The second aspect of federal control stems from decisions of the courts. The Supreme Court has had considerable influence on education through a number of major decisions. The 1954 decision on integration of the races in public schools is a notable example of such decisions. The decision holding the Dartmouth College charter to be inviolate is an earlier example of such influence. Supreme Court decisions have not been directly aimed at education in many cases but they have generally dealt with rights of individuals which were in question because of some educational practice. The principle that the state in discharging its responsibilities for schools and control over schools cannot establish or condone practices which deny individuals their constitutional rights has been well-established by these decisions.

There is no clear-cut policy which either clarifies current practice with respect to the control of education or sets forth any theory of appropriate control as related to the three levels of government.

The Issue of Financial Support

States have accepted responsibility for financing schools in their constitutions. There has been no disposition to shirk this responsibility, at least in theory, it being viewed as a normal way to discharge the states' functions with respect to education. The federal government has no such responsibility except such as it may choose to exercise.

Local school districts are given responsibility by the states for financing schools. These responsibilities may be both mandatory and permissive. It is of interest to note that in some states the extent to which the local district can support schools is limited by constitutional enactment where the property tax is the source of support. Mandatory provisions for actually exercising the powers given local districts vary from state to state.

The federal government, on the other hand, has had complete freedom to determine whether or not it chose to support education financially and, if so, for what ends. As has been stated, the government early established the precedent for such support and has steadily strengthened this precedent. There is now a national com-

mitment to education which is expressed in considerable financial
support from the federal level. There is strong opposition to this
concept because it has resulted in limiting support and in the preser-
vation of the established principle of earmarked grants. Nevertheless, the precedent of federal support is so strong that it now has
the effect of an accepted principle of responsibility.

Controversy exists over the question of federal support, the extent
of state support, and the degree of responsibility of local school districts for support. Points of view range from strong convictions
that the federal government should provide no support for schools
to the belief that local communities should provide their own
schools with a minimum of state support or no state support at all.

The issue of support is one of the most crucial issues in government relations to education. There is and has been at no time a
generally accepted policy which clearly identifies the extent of
government responsibility for financial support of schools or the
appropriate sharing of such responsibility by the three levels of
government.

The Issue of Education Goals

The role of government in determining educational goals has
always been evident. The allocation to the government of responsibility for education was initially predicated on assumptions concerning educational purpose inasmuch as schools were viewed as
means to an end and not as ends in themselves. The fact that many
state constitutions are fairly specific in their definition of educational
purpose shows where the locus of responsibility for determining
goals lies.

However, legislative enactments have seldom dealt with the problem of goals in any comprehensive fashion; rather, the approach
has been to stress the specific with little reference to the overall ends
sought. Legislatures have not been inclined to view programs of
financial support in their true relationship to educational goals.

Local districts have been scarcely more diligent in the matter of
determining clear-cut educational goals which are understood and
accepted by the community. The weight of tradition rests heavily
at both levels but current forces which sometimes exert pressure
on the schools may influence change in educational goals—some-

times ill-advised change. Adequate freedom exists on the local level for the vigorous study and definition of directions educational programs should take.

As indicated earlier, federal participation in the setting of goals has been generally limited to the support of selected phases of school programs. There has been no comprehensive approach to influencing educational objectives from the federal level. The appropriation of funds to support selected areas of education has clearly influenced goals but in a somewhat indirect way, even though the final decision on whether or not such support should be accepted remains with the state.

While the state has authority to determine educational goals, there is no clear-cut policy on the exercise of this authority. Both local districts and the federal government have had a definite impact on educational goals. Substantial disagreement exists in the country on the role which education should play in our society. These differences come to the fore when educational problems and issues are considered.

The basic issue of what our educational goals should be and who should determine them is perhaps a perennial one and likely will remain with us.

The Issue of Equality of Opportunity

One of our nation's cherished goals has been the provision of equal opportunities for all to secure an education. Perhaps the issue is not now as much a philisophical one as one of actually providing this opportunity. However, the meaning of the term *equality of opportunity* is still subject to debate. The generally accepted point of view seems to be that the same kinds of education for all do not provide desired equality of opportunity, but rather that each individual should have the kind of education which will be most useful to him in developing his interests and abilities. For example, adequate programs for the mentally retarded and adequate programs for the gifted would provide equal opportunity but the same program for both would not.

As a nation, we have yet to decide how much education and what quality is needed in order to provide equality of opportunity and to safeguard the best interests of our society. Heretofore, equalization has rested on court and legislative decisions within states with the result that some states have gone much further in equalizing opportunity than have others. When equality of opportunity is defined by each of the states, significant variations in the level of equality of opportunity are prevelant. Measured by the factor of financial support, the states which define the highest level of minimum educational opportunity exceed the minimum level defined by the poorest states by as much as 300 per cent. Furthermore, wide variations in educational opportunity still exist within states.

The mobility of population and the interrelationships within our society pose serious questions concerning whether or not the determination of equality of opportunity should be left entirely to the states because they differ so widely in ability and willingness to provide education.

The only authority for achieving general equality of opportunity resides with the federal government. The argument has been advanced and vigorously supported that herein lies the true role of the national government in education. It has been argued that the power to tax the entire nation should be utilized for the support of education and that the distribution of revenues should be on the basis of providing a minimum level of opportunity for all within the fifty states.

There are two parts to this issue: What level and quality of educational opportunity is needed for all and how should this level and quality be provided?

The Issue of Support for
Nonpublic Schools

Private and parochial schools are older than public institutions of learning. As increased government support has strengthened public schools, the issue of whether public funds should be made available to nonpublic schools has been brought into sharper focus. Nonpublic schools have sought public support on the grounds that their programs and services are in the interest of the general welfare just as are those of the public schools. However, a segment of the purposes of parochial schools deals with the religious goals which their church seeks to serve.

Precedents have been established by decisions of the Supreme

Court upholding the allocation of public funds for support of school transportation, school lunch services, and instructional materials in nonpublic schools on the grounds that such aid goes to the student rather than to the school. Newer areas of federal support, such as the National Defense Education Act and loans for building construction to institutions of higher learning have provided additional opportunities to sharpen this issue. Any time a general aid bill is introduced in Congress the issue comes to the forefront. The amount of public support going into nonpublic schools has been increasing within recent years.

The major question revolves around the broader issues of separation of church and state. The meanings of this doctrine with respect to education are not clear at this time. It is difficult to see how the federal court can rule that a prayer endorsed by a board of education cannot be used in the public schools on the grounds that it violates the doctrine of separation of church and state while, on the other hand, public funds are used to support nonpublic school programs.

The increasing number of court decisions on this issue indicates its growing importance.

Stated simply, the question is: What is the meaning of separation of church and state as applied to state support of nonpublic schools?

Summary

The steadily increasing role of government in education is clear from the foregoing pages. Legislative, executive, and judicial branches of government each find themselves more and more concerned with the public schools and their programs. Recognized relationships of education to individual and social well-being, the growing complexity of our society, and the use of education for national survival account for these trends.

Decentralization of education, the division of responsibility, control and support among the various levels and branches of government, while consistent with the historical role ascribed to education in America, have posed vexing problems and issues. While important guides to the proper role of government in education have evolved from experience, troublesome issues remain to be resolved.

Among these issues are the following: Who shall control education? What shall be our educational goals? How shall these goals be determined? How shall education be financed? What is the meaning of equality of educational opportunity and how shall such equality be achieved? What is the meaning of the doctrine of separation of church and state with respect to education? What are the proper roles of the various levels and branches of government in education? What are the proper interrelationships of these roles.

The resolution of these issues depends in large measure on decisions made through the various levels and branches of government.

Bibliography

Beach, Fred F.,and Robert F. Will, *The State and Education*. U.S. Department of Health, Education, and Welfare, Misc. No. 23. Washington, D.C.: Office of Education, 1955. 175 pp.

————, *The State and Nonpublic Schools*. U.S. Department of Health, Education, and Welfare. Washington, D.C.: Office of Education, 1958. 152 pp.

Cummings, Howard H.,and Helen K. Mackintosh, *Curriculum Responsibilities of State Departments of Education*. U.S. Department of Health, Education, and Welfare. Washington, D.C.: Office of Education, 1960. 76 pp.

Edwards, Newton, *The Courts and The Public Schools*. Chicago: The University of Chicago Press, 1955. 622 pp.

Grieder, Calvin, Truman M. Pierce, and William Everett Rosenstengel, *Public School Administration*. 2nd ed. New York: The Ronald Press Company, 1961. 642 pp.

Harris, Chester W., ed. *Encyclopedia of Educational Research*. New York: The Macmillan Company, 1960.

Hutchins, Clayton B.,and Delores A. Steinhilber, *Trends in Financing Public Education, 1929–30 to 1959–60*. U.S. Department of Health, Education, and Welfare. Washington, D.C.: Office of Education, 1961.

Johns, Roe L.,and Edgar L. Morphet, *Financing the Public Schools*. Englewood Cliffs, N.J.: Prentice-Hall, Inc., 1960. 566 pp.

Martorana, S. V.,and Ernest V. Hollis, *Survey of State Legislation Relating to Higher Education*. U.S. Department of Health, Education, and Welfare. Washington, D.C.: Office of Education, 1962. 273 pp.

Morphet, Edgar L., Roe L. Johns, and Theodore L. Reller, *Educational Administration, Concepts, Practices, and Issues*. Englewood Cliffs, N.J.: Prentice-Hall, Inc., 1959.

Munse, Albert R., Eugene P. McLoone, and Clayton D. Hutchins, *Public School Finance Programs of the United States, 1957–58*. U.S. Department of Health, Education, and Welfare. Washington, D.C.: Office of Education, 1960.

Munse, Albert R., *Revenue Programs for the Public Schools in the United States, 1959–60*. U.S. Department of Health, Education, and Welfare. Washington, D.C.: Office of Education, 1961.

Quattlebaum, Charles A., *Federal Educational Policies, Programs and Proposals*, Parts I, II, and III. A Survey and Handbook Prepared in The Legislative Reference Service of the Library of Congress. Washington, D.C.: Government Printing Office, 1960.

Spurlock, Clark, *Education and the Supreme Court*. Urbana, Ill.: University of Illinois, 1955. 252 pp.

The Pupil's Day in Court: Review of 1961. Research Division, National Education Association. Washington, D.C.: The Association, 1961. 56 pp.

Index